AN INSPECTOR CALLS

J.B. PRIESTLEY

NOTES BY JOHN SCICLUNA

Longman  York Press

YORK PRESS
322 Old Brompton Road, London SW5 9JH

PEARSON EDUCATION LIMITED
Edinburgh Gate, Harlow,
Essex CM20 2JE, United Kingdom
Associated companies, branches and representatives throughout the world

First published 1997
This new and fully revised edition first published 2002
Second impression 2003

10 9 8 7 6 5 4 3 2

ISBN 0 582 50625 5

Designed by Michelle Cannatella
Illustrations by Susan Smith
Phototypeset by Gem Graphics, Trenance, Mawgan Porth, Cornwall
Colour reproduction and film output by Spectrum Colour
Produced by Pearson Education North Asia Limited, Hong Kong

CONTENTS

PART ONE
INTRODUCTION

PART TWO
SUMMARIES

PART THREE
COMMENTARY

PART FOUR
RESOURCES

Preface

York Notes are designed to give you a broader perspective on works of literature studied at GCSE and equivalent levels. With examination requirements changing in the twenty-first century, we have made a number of significant changes to this new series. We continue to help students to reach their own interpretations of the text but York Notes now have important extra-value new features.

You will discover that York Notes are genuinely interactive. The new **Checkpoint** features make sure that you can test your knowledge and broaden your understanding. You will also be directed to excellent websites, books and films where you can follow up ideas for yourself.

The **Resources** section has been updated and an entirely new section has been devoted to how to improve your grade. Careful reading and application of the principles laid out in the Resources section guarantee improved performance.

The **Detailed summaries** include an easy-to-follow skeleton structure of the story-line, while the section on **Language and style** has been extended to offer an in-depth discussion of the writer's techniques.

The Contents page shows the structure of this study guide. However, there is no need to read from the beginning to the end as you would with a novel, play or poem. Use the Notes in the way that suits you. Our aim is to help you with your understanding of the work, not to dictate how you should learn.

Our authors are practising English teachers and examiners who have used their experience to offer a whole range of **Examiner's secrets** – useful hints to encourage exam success.

The General Editor of this series is John Polley, Senior GCSE Examiner and former Head of English at Harrow Way Community School, Andover.

The author of these Notes is John Scicluna, who, having studied English and Drama, began teaching in 1967. Since that time he has been actively involved in the teaching of English and English Literature to secondary-age pupils.

The text used in these Notes is the Heinemann Plays edition, 1992, with an introduction and notes by Tim Bezant. Page numbering is the same as in the earlier Hereford edition.

INTRODUCTION

HOW TO STUDY A PLAY

Though it may seem obvious, remember that a play is written to be performed before an audience. Ideally, you should see the play live on stage. A film or video recording is next best, though neither can capture the enjoyment of being in a theatre and realising that your reactions are part of the performance.

There are six aspects of a play:

1. THE PLOT: a play is a story whose events are carefully organised by the playwright in order to show how a situation can be worked out
2. THE CHARACTERS: these are the people who have to face this situation. Since they are human they can be good or bad, clever or stupid, likeable or detestable, etc. They may change too!
3. THE THEMES: these are the underlying messages of the play, e.g. jealousy can cause the worst of crimes; ambition can bring the mightiest low
4. THE SETTING: this concerns the time and place that the author has chosen for the play
5. THE LANGUAGE: the writer uses a certain style of expression to convey the characters and ideas
6. STAGING AND PERFORMANCE: the type of stage, the lighting, the sound effects, the costumes, the acting styles and delivery must all be decided

Work out the choices the dramatist has made in the first four areas, and consider how a director might balance these choices to create a live performance.

The purpose of these York Notes is to help you understand what the play is about and to enable you to make your own interpretation. Do not expect the study of a play to be neat and easy: plays are chosen for examination purposes, not written for them!

EXAMINER'S SECRET

In an exam take the time to read questions carefully. A few minutes quiet reading can also calm the nerves!

AUTHOR – LIFE AND WORKS

1894 John Boynton Priestley born, 13 September, in Bradford Yorkshire

1910 Priestley leaves school and takes a job with a firm of wool merchants

1914–18 Priestley joins 10th Duke of Wellington's Regiment. Serves on front line in France. Is wounded and gassed

1919 Awarded a place at Trinity Hall, Cambridge, to study literature, history and political science

1921 Marries Pat Tempest, a young woman he met in Bradford

1922 Begins work in London as journalist writing for publications such as *The Times Literary Supplement* and *The New Statesman*

1922 Publishes his first collection of essays under the title *Brief Diversions*

1925 *The English Comic Character* is published

1925 His first wife, Pat Priestley, dies of cancer

1926 Marries Jane Wyndham Lewis, with whom he had been having an affair during Pat's illness, and by whom he already had a daughter, Mary

CONTEXT

1892 Keir Hardy stands as Independent Labour candidate and is elected as the country's first socialist M.P.

1901 Death of Queen Victoria. Her son becomes King Edward VII. Start of the Edwardian era

1906 Labour Party is founded after the success of the Labour Representation Committee in the General Election

1910 Death of King Edward VII

1914–18 First World War

1920 League of Nations has its first meeting. Coal miners strike throughout Britain

1923 German currency collapses

1924 First Labour government formed under Ramsay McDonald

1926 General Strike hits British industry

1928 Equal Franchise Act gives vote to all women over twenty-one

1929 American economy hit by slump and Wall Street Crash

AUTHOR – LIFE AND WORKS

1932 Writes play *Dangerous Corner*

1934 Uses his travels through poorer parts of Britain to write *English Journey*

1937 Writes play *Time and Conways*

1938 Writes *When We Are Married*

1939–40 Makes regular wartime broadcasts on BBC Radio, 1940 radio talks published as *Britain Speaks*

1952 After many affairs, Priestley divorces Jane and marries the writer Jacquetta Hawkes

1957 Writes the article 'Russia, the Atom and the West' in *The New Statesman*; as a result the Campaign for Nuclear Disarmament is formed

1962 Writes *Margin Released*, first volume of his autobiography

1977 Second part of autobiography, *Instead of The Tree* is written

1984 J.B. Priestley dies

CONTEXT

1933 Adolf Hitler, leader of Nazi Party, elected Chancellor of Germany

1939–45 Second World War

1945 Hitler's commits suicide; Germany surrenders; Churchill's wartime coalition government resigns; Labour government formed under Clement Attlee after landslide victory in General Election; Atomic bombs dropped on Japan

1947 British rule in India ends with formation of the dominions of India and Pakistan

1948 Indian pacifist leader Mahatma Gandhi is assassinated; British Nation Health Service is founded

1949 De Havilland Comet, the world's first jet airliner, makes its maiden flight

1957 Treaty of Rome creates European Common Market, forerunner of present European Community

1961 Yuri Gagarin becomes first man in space

1969 Neil Armstrong is the first man to walk on the moon

1984 First 'free' walk in space from the US shuttle Challenger; miners strike in British coalfields; Indian troops attack Sikh Golden Temple at Amritsar; IRA bomb explodes at Tory Party Conference in Brighton; Mrs Gandhi, Prime Minister of India, is shot dead

SETTING AND BACKGROUND

A PRE-FIRST WORLD WAR SETTING

The setting of *An Inspector Calls* is important in a number of ways. J.B. Priestley sets the play in the fictional industrial city of Brumley. Brumley is probably typical of many towns where the factory owners, who provided much-needed employment, were able to run things pretty much as they wanted. Although it is a fictional place, J.B. Priestley gives us quite a lot of information about it.

The importance of the town is indicated by its having a Lord Mayor and a police force with its own Chief Constable. Arthur Birling clearly feels that his activities in local politics have made him enough of a figure to justify his being given a knighthood. The number of women who are poor and in need of help is suggested by the existence of the Brumley Women's Charity Organisation with which Mrs Birling is involved. It is interesting to notice that whether someone got help or not could depend on whether the organisers, like Mrs Birling, thought that person deserved to be helped or whether they thought that the person deserved to suffer.

Before the First World War the majority of working women worked as domestic servants.

By mentioning men like Alderman Meggarty, J.B. Priestley was making a general point about a time when the underprivileged and powerless are made the victims of the privileged and powerful. By setting the play before the First World War, J.B. Priestley could make the most of these social divisions.

STAGING

All action of the play takes place in the Birling's dining room, which is described as '*substantial and heavily comfortable, but not cosy and homelike*' (Act I, p. 1), which reflects the family's outward comfort and inner tensions. The realistic stage set has another function. J.B. Priestley liked to begin his plays by convincing his audiences that they were safely within the boundaries of what was real and normal – and then he would find a way to destroy that feeling of reality and move them into an unreal or mysterious situation. By using the solid and naturalistic stage setting Priestley gives his audience a sense of reality while the mysterious role of the Inspector and the time-switch at the end of the play introduce contrasting, unreal elements.

SOCIAL AND HISTORICAL CONTEXT

The social and historical context of the play are equally important. Social position was far more important than it is today. Following the dramatic expansion of industry throughout the nineteenth century, many men who had invested in such industries as coal, iron and steel, pottery and textiles had made considerable fortunes. Men such as Arthur Birling may have come from humble origins but their wealth allowed them to rise up the social ladder. Marriages between these newly rich families and aristocratic, but often impoverished land-owning families, helped to secure new social positions. Many of these industrialists were granted titles and this too helped to improve their social standing.

You will gain more credit if you show you have some understanding of the play in its historical context.

The Labour Party, founded by James Keir Hardie in 1893, was only just beginning to make an impact on the political life of the country. The rights of workers, like Eva Smith, were not taken too seriously by many employers, but at the same time many working people had benefited from the generosity of those industrialists who genuinely cared for the welfare of their workers, even to the extent of building idealistic new towns for them to live in.

Men like Arthur Birling could be seen as a throwback to harsh early Victorian times, but sadly he may have been all too typical of the greedy employers of that time. Life might have been good for him, but it was not good for his workers. Although King Edward VII died in 1910, the time from his accession to the throne in 1901 and the start of the First World War in 1914 is usually referred to as the Edwardian Era. To many people, and J.B. Priestley may have been such a person, the end of the Edwardian era and the onset of the war marked an end to a time of peace and stability, and harking back nostalgically to it can be a sort of escape from an unpleasant and uncertain future.

Yet the Edwardian era was a period of false security. In his play *Eden End* which he also set in 1912, J.B. Priestley has one of his major characters say 'the world's got a lot more sense than it's given credit for in the newspapers. And it's got science to help it'. J.B. Priestley wrote *Eden End* in 1934 and there is a clear message against the complacent attitude that so many were showing towards the rise of the dictators in Germany, Italy, Spain and the Soviet Union. Similarly in *An Inspector Calls*, Mr Birling looks to a prosperous future without wars, a future where technology will bring progress unspoiled by social problems.

Just as in 1934 when J.B. Priestley was warning against the rise of European dictators, so in 1945 (when *An Inspector Calls* was actually written) he is warning of the consequences of not making the social changes that natural justice demanded. J.B. Priestley had fought in the First World War and had seen the soldiers, who had been promised that they would return to a 'fit country for heroes to live in' (David Lloyd George, 1918), returning home to the grim reality of unemployment, recession, strikes and hunger marches. He would surely have wanted something more worthwhile and honourable when the new Labour government with its promise of a Welfare State swept to victory after the horrors of the Second World War.

Now take a break! 

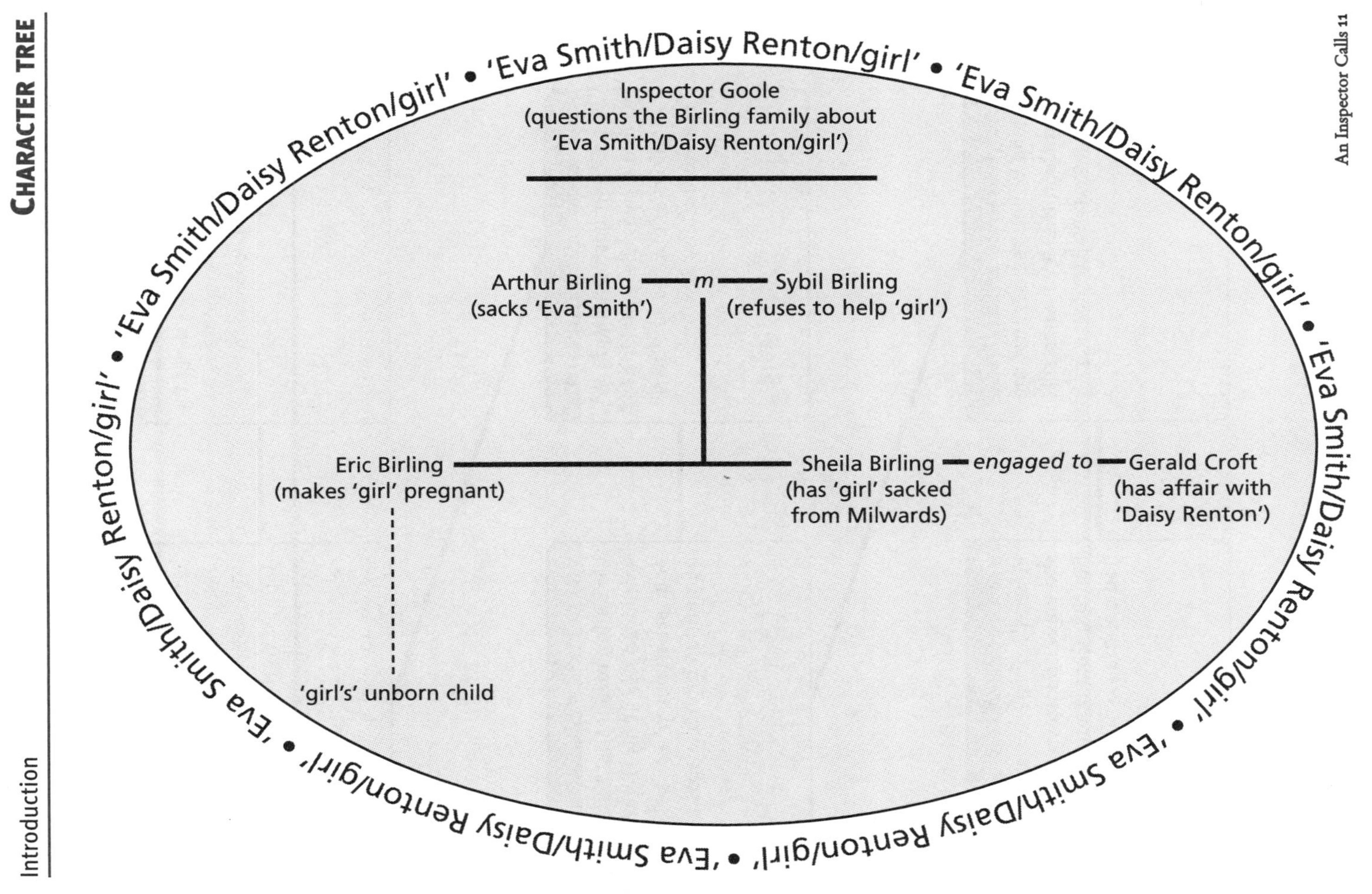
'Eva Smith/Daisy Renton/girl' • 'Eva Smith/Daisy Renton/girl' • 'Eva Smith/Daisy Renton/girl' • 'Eva Smith/Daisy Renton/girl' • 'Eva Smith/Daisy Renton/girl' • 'Eva Smith/Daisy Renton/girl' • 'Eva Smith/Daisy Renton/girl' • 'Eva Smith/Daisy Renton/girl'
Inspector Goole
(questions the Birling family about
'Eva Smith/Daisy Renton/girl')
Arthur Birling
(sacks 'Eva Smith')
m
Sybil Birling
(refuses to help 'girl')
Eric Birling
(makes 'girl' pregnant)
Sheila Birling
(has 'girl' sacked
from Milwards)
engaged to
Gerald Croft
(has affair with
'Daisy Renton')
'girl's' unborn child

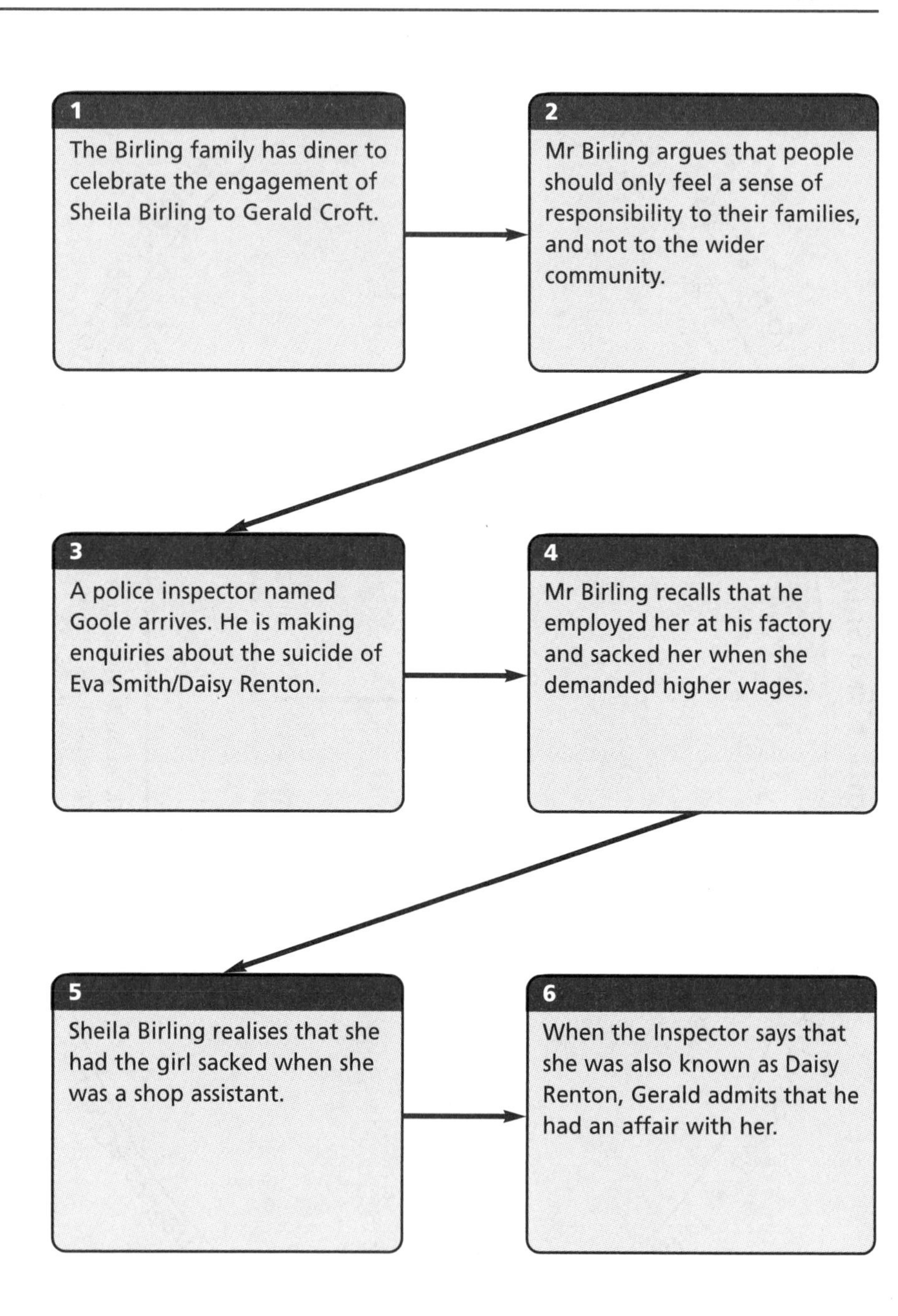
1
The Birling family has diner to celebrate the engagement of Sheila Birling to Gerald Croft.
2
Mr Birling argues that people should only feel a sense of responsibility to their families, and not to the wider community.
3
A police inspector named Goole arrives. He is making enquiries about the suicide of Eva Smith/Daisy Renton.
4
Mr Birling recalls that he employed her at his factory and sacked her when she demanded higher wages.
5
Sheila Birling realises that she had the girl sacked when she was a shop assistant.
6
When the Inspector says that she was also known as Daisy Renton, Gerald admits that he had an affair with her.

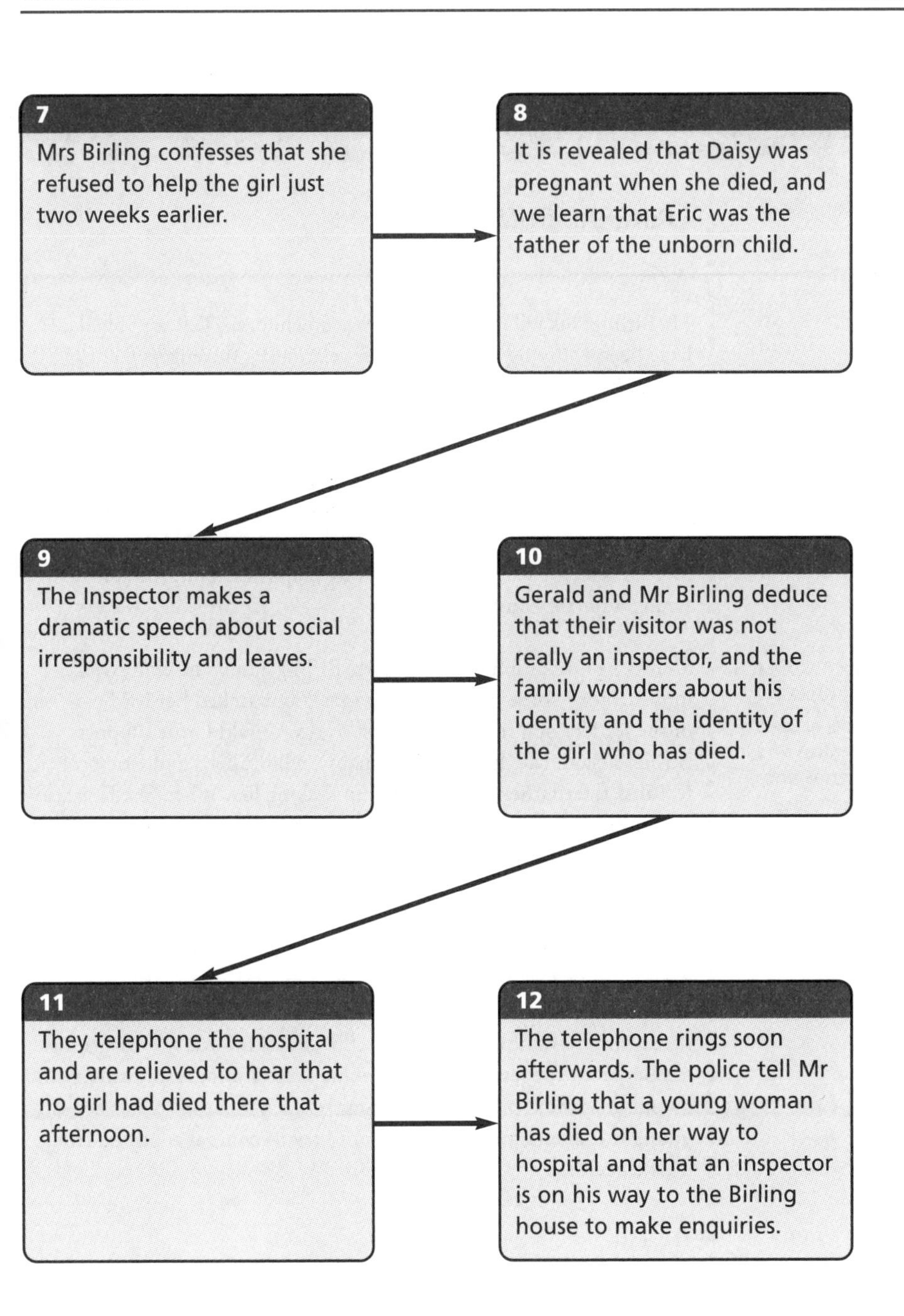
7
Mrs Birling confesses that she refused to help the girl just two weeks earlier.
8
It is revealed that Daisy was pregnant when she died, and we learn that Eric was the father of the unborn child.
9
The Inspector makes a dramatic speech about social irresponsibility and leaves.
10
Gerald and Mr Birling deduce that their visitor was not really an inspector, and the family wonders about his identity and the identity of the girl who has died.
11
They telephone the hospital and are relieved to hear that no girl had died there that afternoon.
12
The telephone rings soon afterwards. The police tell Mr Birling that a young woman has died on her way to hospital and that an inspector is on his way to the Birling house to make enquiries.

SUMMARIES

GENERAL SUMMARY

ACT I

Mr Birling, his wife and their grown-up children, Eric and Sheila, have been enjoying a family dinner celebrating the engagement of Sheila Birling to Gerald Croft. In an expansive mood, Mr Birling makes pompous speeches outlining his views on technology and industrial relations. He says that a man only needs to care for himself and his family and that they should ignore the 'cranks' (p. 10) who claim that everybody has a responsibility to care for everybody else in the community. The evening is interrupted by the arrival of a police inspector named Goole making enquiries about the suicide of a young woman, Eva Smith.

EXAMINER'S SECRET

Familiarise youself with technical and literary terms and use them in your answers.

Shown a photograph of the girl, Mr Birling admits he employed her in his factory some two years previously but sacked her for being one of the leaders of a strike for higher wages. Gerald Croft supports Birling's claim that he acted reasonably, while Sheila and Eric both feel that their father acted harshly in sacking her. When Sheila is also shown the photograph she realises that, driven by jealousy and ill temper, she later had the same girl sacked from her job as a shop assistant.

The Inspector appears to have an uncanny knowledge of the family's dealings with Eva Smith. When he announces that the girl had changed her name to Daisy Renton, Gerald's reaction makes it clear that he too has known the girl. By the end of the Act the Inspector has begun to suggest that many people share a joint responsibility for the misery which prompted Eva Smith/Daisy Renton to end her sad young life. Sheila warns Gerald not to try to conceal anything from the Inspector.

ACT II

The strain of the earlier part of the evening is evident in the tension between Sheila and Gerald. Gerald admits that in the spring of the previous year he met Daisy Renton and she became his mistress. He ended the affair some six months later. Sheila is hurt and angry at Gerald's involvement with the girl, yet she feels a certain respect for the openness of his admission.

Despite Mrs Birling's attempts to intimidate the Inspector and to control events, Sheila's feeling that it is foolish to try to hinder his enquiries appears increasingly well founded. Sheila is concerned that her mother will also be implicated in the girl's suffering. While Eric is out of the room, despite her blustering, Mrs Birling is forced to admit that just two weeks earlier the girl tried to get help from Mrs Birling and was refused. It is revealed that the girl was pregnant and there is now a strong suspicion that Eric might was the father of that unborn child.

When you are revising it is a good idea to take regular breaks. Most of us can really only concentrate fully for between 25 and 30 minutes.

ACT III

Eric confesses that he got the girl pregnant. He also stole money from his father's firm to try to support her. Eric is horrified to learn that his mother refused to help the girl and he blames his mother for the death of the girl and of the unborn child. Any pretence at family unity starts to dissolve. The Inspector has done his job and shown that each of them had a part in ruining the girl's life. He makes a dramatic speech about the consequences of the sort of social irresponsibility that Mr Birling was preaching at the end of the dinner, and he leaves.

Between them Gerald and Mr Birling are gradually able to prove that the man was not a real police inspector. This raises a doubt about whether they have really all been talking about the same girl – and about whether any girl has actually killed herself. A telephone call to the Infirmary confirms that there is no record of any girl dying there that afternoon. There is a general feeling of relief at this information. Sheila and Eric still feel guilty for their actions and they seem to have been changed for the better by what has happened. The others feel a greater sense of relief; their confidence and belief in the rightness of their actions is restored. At this point the telephone rings. Mr Birling answers it to find that it is the police calling. He is told that a young woman has just died on her way to the Infirmary and an inspector is on his way to make enquiries into her death.

PALE ALE

Detailed summaries

Part one [pp. 1–7] – The dinner party

CHECKPOINT 1

What do we learn of Mr Birling's attitudes towards marriage and society?

1. **The Birling family and Gerald Croft are enjoying a dinner to celebrate the engagement of Gerald to Sheila.**
2. **Mr Birling makes a speech congratulating the engaged couple and expressing the hope that their marriage will lead to closer and more profitable links between the firms owned by the Birling and Croft families.**
3. **Gerald presents Sheila with an engagement ring.**
4. **The ladies leave the room while the men enjoy port and cigars.**

EXAMINER'S SECRET

The examiner will be impressed if you use quotations from the play to back up your points – but make sure your quotations are accurate!

In his **stage directions**, J.B. Priestley takes care to set the scene in the large house of a wealthy businessman. He briefly describes the four members of the Birling family and their guest, Gerald Croft. A meal celebrating the engagement of Gerald Croft to Sheila Birling is just ending. The port is passed round and glasses are filled for a toast wishing the happy couple 'the very best that life can bring' (p. 4). The toast is drunk, and Gerald chooses his moment to present Sheila with an engagement ring.

CHECKPOINT 2

What are our immediate impressions of Mr Birling? Consider the views he expresses.

The solid and substantial house, the champagne glasses, decanter of port and the cigars reflect the comfortable, rich lifestyle of the well-respected Birling family.

The easy, light-hearted conversation shows Sheila as excitable, youthful and enthusiastic, while Eric seems shy, awkward and close to getting drunk. Gerald appears self-assured and someone who knows how to behave at all times. Mrs Birling takes little part in the conversation and what she does say reinforces the idea that she is a cold person who stands apart from others. Mr Birling, by contrast, is in a good mood but cannot resist making speeches. He says he is confident that the future will bring peace and prosperity, with 'Capital' and 'Labour' (p. 7) working together. He condemns 'Bernard Shaw', 'H.G. Wellses' (p. 7) and others with Socialist views. His comments show how wrong he can be: the *Titanic* would sink on its maiden voyage; there would be two World Wars; depression, social unrest, unemployment and strikes would characterise the next three decades.

DID YOU KNOW?

Titanic was owned by the White Star company. When she was launched she was the largest ship afloat and it was thought that she was unsinkable. She sank on her maiden voyage after hitting an iceberg, on 14 April 1912, and some 1,500 people lost their lives.

Mr Birling's views on technology and the future

Birling's speech emphasises his confidence that the future will bring good times to manufacturers like them with fewer strikes and greater prosperity. He talks about advances in technology, quoting the newly launched *Titanic* as a symbol of progress. He says that by 1940 the world will be a place of peace and prosperity, with strikes and wars as things of the past. He says it is important for sensible businessmen to speak out against socialist ideas.

As the play goes on, the audience of course will regard Birling's later pronouncements with suspicion since the views he expresses here are so clearly wrong.

GLOSSARY

Capital Birling uses the word to represent those who owned the factories

Labour Birling refers here to employed working people rather than the political Labour Party

Bernard Shaw and H.G. Wells both of these famous writers had an interest in social justice and the socialist cause – as did J.B. Priestley himself

PART TWO [pp. 7–11] – Mr Birling confides in Gerald

1 Gerald remains in the dining room with Mr Birling who is worried about what Gerald's mother thinks of the family.

2 Mr Birling tells Gerald there is a chance of his getting a knighthood in the New Year's Honours list.

3 Gerald and Mr Birling joke about a scandal ruining that possibility.

4 Eric returns and tells them the women are talking about clothes so there is no hurry.

5 Mr Birling states that a man's only responsibility is to himself and his family. He scoffs at the notion of responsibility to others in society.

6 He is interrupted by someone at the front door.

CHECKPOINT 3

How does Mr Birling appear to be closer to Gerald than to his own son?

DID YOU KNOW?

Many people in the past have bought knighthoods and other honours by making donations to whichever political party was in power!

When the two man are left alone, Birling expresses his concern that Lady Croft (Gerald's mother) fears that the Birling family are socially inferior. To put Gerald's mind at ease, Birling confides that there is a strong possibility that he will be knighted in the next Honours List.

Birling sees a knighthood as a fair reward for his involvement as 'a sound useful party man' (p. 8) in local politics, as well as a way for him to become an equal of Sir George Croft.

Apart from the superiority that Sir George has because of his title, Lady Croft's family come from the land-owning gentry. Birling is clearly concerned that his place in society depends on his acquired wealth rather than on good family connections.

J.B. Priestley shows us how superficial the honours system can be when Birling's faithful support of a political party counts so highly towards his gaining a knighthood. Birling is happy to accept the community's reward in the form of a knighthood, but his speech shows that he regards real commitment to the community as being nonsense.

Challenging Birling

Birling's views on society – 'community and all that nonsense' (p. 10) – are challenged by the arrival of the Inspector.

It is particularly striking that the family's feeling of self-satisfaction shown by Birling's comments about responsibility coincide with the moment of the Inspector's arrival. This is **ironic** since the Inspector is there to try to teach them all something about the real responsibility they have towards other people.

CHECKPOINT 4

In the course of the play how does Priestley develop the idea of events in time being like links in a chain?

PART THREE [pp. 11–16] – The enquiry begins

1. **Birling tries to take control, mentioning his long service in local government and his position as a magistrate.**
2. **The Inspector is unimpressed and says he has come to make enquiries about a girl who has died in the 'Infirmary' (p. 11) after deliberately drinking disinfectant.**
3. **Birling recognises the girl from a photograph which the Inspector produces.**
4. **It turns out that Birling sacked the girl for her part in leading a strike for higher wages.**

The Inspector arrives and is represented as being an incorruptible force for good. He is described as creating a big impression and as being solid and purposeful. His control of the situation and his sincerity contrast sharply with Birling's attitudes.

Birling's relaxed and condescending manner becomes aggressive as he finds himself having to defend his actions.

Birling is a hard-headed businessman who considers that his importance as a former 'alderman' (p. 11) and Lord Mayor, his role as a magistrate, his social position and influential friends make him superior to a mere police inspector.

GLOSSARY

useful party man one who supports a political party and is loyal to its policies
Infirmary hospital
alderman senior member of a town council

CHECKPOINT 5

Compare Mr Birling's attempt to intimidate the Inspector with the way Mrs Birling behaves in Act II (pp. 30–1).

We learn that the girl was called Eva Smith, and we discover something of her background and character. The Inspector declares that even though he sacked the girl nearly two years ago, Birling was still a link in the 'chain of events' (p. 14) leading to her death. Gerald supports Birling's view that it was right to sack the ringleaders. Eric feels his father acted harshly, especially as Birling admits the girl was a good worker who had been considered for promotion. Birling is irritated by Eric's apparent unwillingness to 'face a few responsibilities' (p. 16) which he blames on the 'public-school-and-Varsity life' (p. 16) that Eric has enjoyed. He is also irritated by the Inspector's insinuations, and tries to use his friendship with the 'Chief Constable' (p. 16) to frighten the Inspector. The Inspector remains calm and determined. Birling shrugs off responsibility for the girl's death but is curious as to what happened to her after she was sacked from the factory.

DID YOU KNOW?

The girls at the factory were striking for a rise to bring their wages to 'about twenty-five shillings a week' (p. 14). In our decimal currency that comes to £1.25 per week!

Birling has no sense of loyalty towards his workers. He regarded the strike with contempt and refused to consider the workers' need for more money if it meant he must have less profit. Birling admits that Eva Smith had good qualities, she was lively and a good worker, but he disliked her willingness to voice her opinions. Birling shows his low opinion and lack of concern when he asks the Inspector whether Eva Smith went 'on the streets' (p. 16). Gerald's support of Birling shows that he too cares more for profits than for the welfare of those his company employs.

The role of Eva Smith

Eva Smith does not appear, yet she is central to the developing action of the play. She has left a diary and a letter which give the Inspector the information he needs to follow his chain of events. It is **ironic** that Birling sacked Eva Smith for showing qualities of leadership – the same qualities for which he was earlier prepared to promote her. Since J.B. Priestley makes her case through the Inspector, who is a sympathetic character; we feel he too is sympathetic towards her.

CHECKPOINT 6

What information does the inspector give us about Eva Smith in Act I?

PART FOUR [pp. 16–21] – Sheila's sympathy turns to shock

1. **When Sheila returns, Birling thinks their business with the Inspector has ended.**
2. **The Inspector annoys Birling by continuing his enquiries.**
3. **Sheila is shocked by the description of the girl's suicide.**
4. **Birling becomes less aggressive when he realises that others in the family might know something of the girl's life.**
5. **Sheila becomes agitated on hearing the girl was sacked from Milwards.**
6. **Shown a photograph, Sheila runs from the room crying.**

Birling again ridicules the idea that his sacking of the girl two years earlier could have had any link to her death. Eric feels there might be a connection and Sheila feels sympathy for the girl. Sheila agrees with the Inspector that girls like Eva Smith 'aren't cheap labour – they're *people*' (p. 19), but Gerald again supports Birling's view.

Birling senses a possible scandal and, wishing to avoid any public unpleasantness, tries to settle things quietly with the Inspector. Sheila is curious, but the name Eva Smith means nothing to her. The

GLOSSARY

public-school-and Varsity Eric had the privileges of being educated in a fee-paying school and of going to university

Chief Constable the senior officer in charge of a county or municipal police force

[go] on the streets become a prostitute

Inspector tells them that she changed her name after she was sacked from Birlings, that she was out of work for two months and was feeling desperate till she had the good fortune to have 'a wonderful stroke of luck' (p. 20) working in a dress shop. She had done well there for a time but a complaint from a customer had forced her employer to sack her.

CHECK THE NET

You can find information on J.B. Priestley on the website **www.jbpriestley-society.com**

The Inspector begins to draw others into the tragedy of Eva Smith's life and death. He attracts the sympathy of Sheila and of the audience by his clear and hard-hitting description of the girl's misery. That sympathy for the girl is added to by the details of her pleasant appearance, the poverty she suffered from the loss of her job at Birlings and by the absence of relatives to help her when she was in trouble.

CHECKPOINT 7

In what ways might Sheila's treatment of the girl be said to be more cruel than Mr Birling's treatment of her?

The girl is shown to have been a victim of circumstance. She lost her jobs at Birlings and at Milwards for reasons which J.B. Priestley intends the audience to feel were harsh and unjustified.

Sheila's initial distress at having her happy evening spoiled by the sad news serves to reflect the greater unhappiness of the dead girl's life and to foreshadow the greater distress that Sheila will feel when she sees the photograph.

Through the Inspector's comments on the way that factory owners exploited the desperation of others, J.B. Priestley begins to put across his message about social injustice.

A link in the chain

The careful references to the girl getting a job at Milwards in December (1910) and losing it at the end of January (1911) help to show the timing of events leading to her suicide. We begin to see that the passing of time and when things happen are important to the plot. The careful references to the timing of the events helps show the links in the 'chain of events' (Act I, p. 14) which the Inspector sets out to establish.

PART FIVE [pp. 21–6] – Sheila and the shop girl

1. **Birling is angry with the Inspector for upsetting Sheila, and he goes out to tell his wife what is happening.**
2. **Sheila returns and confesses that she was the customer who had the girl sacked.**
3. **The Inspector makes Sheila realise what a terrible thing she has done.**
4. **The Inspector reveals the girl had changed her name to Daisy Renton. Gerald reacts sharply to the name.**
5. **Sheila warns Gerald not to try to hide the truth.**

Birling is more concerned that his daughter has been upset than by any feelings of guilt or shame for what they might have done to Eva Smith. He does not yet realise the depth of the family's involvement and still feels able to be angry and outspoken towards the Inspector.

CHECKPOINT 8

Why does Sheila react so strongly to the photograph that she is shown?

The Inspector's comment 'a nasty mess somebody's made of it' (p. 21) shows his increasingly moralistic tone. This leads to his comment 'if it was left to me' (p. 22) which sets him up as a judge, and gives him the authority to state that his enquiries are being

Part five continued

made so that all concerned might try to understand why the girl had died.

Gerald asks to see the photograph, but the Inspector insists on following his enquiries through in his own way and in his own time. The Inspector suggests that there is sometimes little to chose between respectable citizens and criminals.

WWW. CHECK THE NET

You can find listings of books by J.B. Priestley on **www.penguin.co.uk**

Sheila returns and admits she went to Milwards to buy a dress which did not suit her. The pretty shop girl, whom the dress would have suited, smiled. Sheila was angry and jealous. She complained that the girl had been 'impertinent' (p. 24) and insisted that the manager get rid of her. Eric criticises Sheila's behaviour as being 'a bit thick' (p. 24).

The Inspector points out Sheila's petty motives of jealousy and anger, and the misuse of her power as the daughter of rich and influential parents to blackmail the shop into sacking the girl. When he tells Sheila she is only partly to blame we realise he intends that all of them should share the responsibility.

Sheila's regret seems genuine. Although the Inspector will not accept belated regrets as an excuse, Sheila has learnt a lesson and she is determined never to act so unfairly again.

The Inspector sums up what has so far been revealed about the involvement of Birling and Sheila. This gives Priestley an opportunity to recap and keep the audience aware of the way events are developing.

A play has a number of high points – look for where a series of actions leads to a dramatic climax.

The Inspector tells them that Eva changed her name to Daisy Renton. Gerald's reaction to the name Daisy Renton is as clear a sign of recognition as was Sheila's earlier reaction to the photograph. He is the only one whose reaction is triggered only by a name, which suggests that he had a very close relationship with her. He feels that since he is no longer seeing the girl everything is all right, but Sheila has an understanding of the Inspector's power to make them reveal all.

While Eric takes the Inspector to find Mr Birling, Sheila challenges Gerald. She realises that Gerald's lack of attention to her the previous summer was because he was having an affair with Daisy Renton. Gerald tries to deny it. He then admits he knew Daisy Renton, but says he has not seen her for six months. Sheila advises Gerald not to try to fool the Inspector. The Inspector returns.

CHECKPOINT 9

How have Sheila's feelings about herself and about Gerald, changed during the last part of this Act?

The power of the Inspector

Sheila's sense of the Inspector's power is shown when she laughs in a hysterical way and warns Gerald 'Why – you fool – *he knows*. Of course he knows. And I hate to think how much he knows that we don't know yet' (p. 26). Priestley informs us that this leaves Gerald '*crushed*' (p. 26). The Inspector's one word question, 'Well?', at the end of the Act raises the Inspector's position to that of someone who is an all-knowing inquisitor. This adds to our sense of mystery as to where the Inspector has got so much detailed knowledge. We also see that in a strange way Sheila is beginning to identify with the Inspector's point of view.

CHECKPOINT 10

Pick out some moments in Act I that you feel show the Inspector's power over other characters.

GLOSSARY

a bit thick shocking
crushed defeated

Test yourself (Act I)

Who says ...?

1 'a man has to mind his own business and look after himself and his own'

....

2 'This young woman, Eva Smith, was a bit out of the ordinary'

....

3 'She'd had a lot to say – far too much – so she had to go'

....

4 'But these girls aren't cheap labour – they're people'

....

About whom?

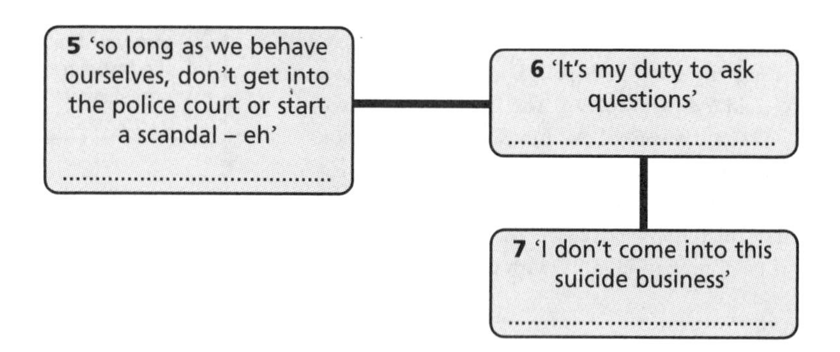

Check your answers on p. 81.

PART ONE [pp. 27–9] – Sharing the guilt

1. **Gerald resents the decision that Sheila should stay to hear the details of his involvement with Daisy Renton.**
2. **The Inspector says that Sheila has accepted her share of responsibility and needs to hear what else happened to the girl so that she does not feel she is the only one who is to blame.**
3. **They agree that sharing something, even blame, is better than not sharing anything.**
4. **Mrs Birling comes in.**

Gerald says he feels Sheila has had a 'long, exciting and tiring day' (p. 27). Gerald suspects that Sheila only wants to stay so that she can see him shamed, just as he had been present to witness her shameful admissions. His excuse that Sheila should be spared the ordeal of listening to his story as it might be 'unpleasant and disturbing' (p. 27) for her, is shown to be hypocritical since Daisy Renton has not been spared what was unpleasant and disturbing for her. The argument between Sheila and Gerald reveals a lack of real trust and understanding in their relationship.

EXAMINER'S SECRET

Read and re-read the play so that you become really familiar with the plot, themes and characters.

The Inspector seems to understand Sheila's feelings in a strange, almost unnatural, way. He does not spare her feelings and his blunt way of describing the circumstances of the girl's death adds to the sense of guilt felt by Sheila and Gerald.

CHECKPOINT 11

How do Sheila's reactions help us question the identity of the Inspector?

The relationship between Sheila and the Inspector

The Inspector's bluntness increases the sense of condemnation that the audience feels for those who have mistreated the girl. Sheila is clearly upset yet we can sense an increasing bond building up between these two characters.

Sheila is struck by the truth of what the Inspector says, even though she cannot properly understand his power or his nature.

CHECK THE NET

J.B. Priestley's family have created a website at **www.jbpriestley.co.uk**

PART TWO [pp. 29–32] – Mrs Birling bustles in

1. **Mrs Birling suspects that Sheila is only motivated by unhealthy curiosity and has no need to stay and be a part of the enquiry.**
2. **She is puzzled when Sheila tries to warn her that the Inspector can break down any defences.**
3. **Mrs Birling tries to impress the Inspector by reminding him of her husband's importance in the community.**
4. **She is shocked when it is revealed that Eric has been regularly drinking far too much.**
5. **She accuses Sheila of being the one who is destroying the family's reputation.**

Mrs Birling feels that the Inspector's attitude and questioning are offensive and 'a trifle impertinent' (p. 30). She believes that she cannot be expected to know anything about 'girls of that class' (p. 30) and is confident that she can handle any questions which are put to her. She tries to show the Inspector how superior she is, but Sheila is aware that her mother has not yet faced being questioned by the Inspector.

We are again reminded of Mr Birling's respected position in the community, but Sheila has already realised that outward respectability is no guarantee of sound moral behaviour.

The Inspector recognises that Sheila and Eric are more easily touched by the sadness of the girl's death. Someone like Mrs Birling, who feels her place in society puts her above such concerns, will clearly be less easily moved. Mr Birling comes in.

J.B. Priestley makes a pointed play on words when the word 'offence' (p. 31) is repeated twice each by Mrs Birling and the Inspector. At first it is used to suggest the possibility of someone being offended, but then there is also the suggestion of the law having been broken and an offence taking place.

The revelations about Eric's drinking habits show us how Mrs Birling prefers to conceal the truth, to build up 'a wall' (p. 32) behind which she and her family can hide. It also helps to prepare us for Eric's admissions about his behaviour towards the girl when he was drunk.

The 'class system' was very strong in England at the beginning of the last century, and it is only recently that people have begun to be genuinely judged on merit.

Don't simply say what happens – comment on *how* and *why*.

Mrs Birling's sense of self-importance

Mrs Birling's sense of her social importance gives her a feeling of security which leads her to treat the Inspector with less respect than the others have done. Her superior tone when she comes in is out of keeping with the apprehension which Sheila and Gerald share as a result of their feelings of responsibility.

PART THREE [pp. 32–40] – Gerald's confession

1. **Mr Birling, who has been trying to persuade Eric to go to bed, is further annoyed by the Inspector's insistence on doing things his own way.**
2. **Gerald makes a feeble attempt to deny any link with the girl.**
3. **He then admits he had met the girl and she had become his mistress.**

GLOSSARY

girls of that class working-class girls, therefore socially inferior to the Birling family

Birling and his wife are startled by the suggestion that Gerald had known Daisy Renton, as the girl was then calling herself. Gerald admits to meeting the girl in 'the stalls bar' of the 'Palace Variety Theatre' (p. 34), a favourite haunt of prostitutes. The girl seemed different from the other 'hard-eyed dough-faced women' (p. 34). She was being pestered by a 'half-drunk and goggle-eyed' (p. 35) local politician and Gerald managed to rescue her from him. He took her to a quiet hotel where they talked. She gave him some vague information about her life and it was clear that she was poor and hungry. He arranged to meet her again two nights later and found her somewhere to live. Her gratitude led to a closer bond between them and they became lovers.

CHECKPOINT 12

How does Gerald's confession contrast with Mr Birling's earlier unwillingness to accept any blame.

Compared to the 'hard-eyed, dough-faced women' (p. 34), Daisy Renton's prettiness and youth make her seem vulnerable. We are more likely to blame Gerald for what happened, even though we can appreciate his motives for rescuing her from Alderman Meggarty. Sheila becomes increasingly sarcastic with Gerald and this could be her way of coping with the revelations about him.

Birling is angry that his daughter is having to hear Gerald's story, but the Inspector supports Sheila's right to hear it. Gerald admits he was flattered by the girl's love and admiration but says he was not in love with her. When he had to go away on business for some weeks he took the opportunity to break off the relationship and gave the girl some money to live on for a time. Although Gerald does not know what became of the girl, the Inspector reveals that her diary showed that she had gone away to a seaside place to enjoy the memory of the happiness she had had with Gerald to remember 'just to make it last longer' (p. 39).

Gerald feels the need to walk in the fresh air after his confession. Sheila gives back his ring. She admits she has been impressed by his honesty but feels that after what they have heard about each other they need to get to know each other over again. Gerald goes out for a walk.

CHECKPOINT 13

How has Gerald's confession affected his relationship with Sheila?

We are made more aware of the Inspector's ability to ask very simple questions and yet to obtain a great deal of information.

Sheila is again seen to be more aware of the Inspector's power to make people confess. She is more deeply influenced by the girl's story and more conscious of the family's responsibility for what has happened.

GLOSSARY

stalls bar a bar on the ground floor of a theatre. The stalls of a variety theatre would have been the cheapest seats

Palace Variety Theatre a theatre which had performances of music, comedy, juggling and dance rather than serious plays

DID YOU KNOW?

J.B. Priestley is careful that the men use **euphemistic** language such as '... Daisy Renton, with other ideas' (p. 33) and 'Women of the town' (p. 34) which hints at prostitution without actually mentioning it. To do otherwise would have offended ladies of 1912.

CHECKPOINT 14

How is the photograph used, and how reliable is it as a piece of evidence?

Links in the chain

Gerald's honest confession helps to add to our knowledge of when things happened to Eva Smith/Daisy Renton. It also makes him a more sympathetic character. Sheila respects his honesty.

The Inspector has already used a photograph to establish the girl's identity, and the 'rough sort of diary' (p. 39) is a convenient device to explain his close knowledge of events.

PART FOUR [pp. 40–2] – Sheila warns her mother

1. **When Sheila comments that Gerald was not shown the photograph, the Inspector points out that it was unnecessary.**
2. **He shows the photograph to Mrs Birling.**
3. **She claims that she does not recognise the girl, and she is angry when the Inspector says that she is lying.**
4. **Birling demands an apology from the Inspector who, instead of apologising, points out that power and influence bring 'responsibilities as well as privileges' (p. 41).**
5. **Sheila advises her mother to tell the truth and not to make things worse.**
6. **The front door slams and Birling goes to see if Eric has left the house.**

Sheila is aware that they must not try to hide behind their respectable reputation. She tells her mother that the Inspector has already got them to admit that the girl was fired by Birling for asking for a reasonable wage, fired from the shop because Sheila was jealous of her and then taken up by Gerald as his mistress and dropped by him. Sheila warns her mother that she is 'making it worse' (p. 42).

EXAMINER'S SECRET

When you have jotted down all the points you wish to use in your examination or coursework essay, take time to organise them carefully.

Sheila is the only one who appreciates the Inspector's power to reveal their dark secrets. Her summary of what has happened to the girl reminds us of the greed, jealousy and selfishness they have shown. Birling and his wife are still trying to use their sense of power and social status to remind the Inspector of his relatively humble social status. The Inspector shows no fear of Birling's importance in the town. He emphasises the ideas of duty and responsibility to suggest the family's lack of such qualities.

The power of the Inspector

The Inspector's sense of assurance again makes us think that he knows everything and that his questions provide the others with an opportunity to admit their faults. Such an admission, as in Gerald's case, can bring the possibility of forgiveness.

PART FIVE [pp. 42–9] – The deserving and the undeserving

1. **Mr Birling returns with the news that Eric has left the house.**
2. **Mrs Birling admits she is a member of the Brumley Women's Charity Organisation, which was set up to help 'women in distress' (p. 42).**

3. **The organisation's committee interviewed the girl two weeks ago.**
4. **Mrs Birling was responsible for the girl being refused help.**
5. **Mrs Birling tells her version of what the girl told the committee.**

CHECKPOINT 15

How does Mrs Birling's attitude, and language, affect our view of her?

It is revealed that the girl appealed to Mrs Birling's organisation for financial help. The girl had called herself Mrs Birling, and this angered the real Mrs Birling who used her influence to ensure that the girl had received no help.

Mrs Birling has a strong sense of how people of different classes should behave. Her prejudice, and dislike of the girl's manner, echo Mr Birling's attitude when he said 'She'd a lot to say – far too much – so she had to go' (Act I, p. 15) and Sheila's anger because the girl was 'very impertinent' (Act I, p. 24). Each used their power and position in order to harm the girl.

Mrs Birling feels no regret for what she did, claiming that she did her duty as the girl had told a pack of lies and so could not be regarded as one of the 'deserving cases' (p. 42). The Inspector reveals that the girl was pregnant and that Mrs Birling knew this. Mrs Birling insisted that the child's father should be the one to help. Sheila is appalled by her mother's heartless attitude, while Mr Birling only seems concerned about the possibility of a public scandal.

Mrs Birling now says that the girl knew who the child's father was but that she would not reveal his name. The girl said that the father had offered to marry her but that she thought he was too immature to take on the responsibility. He had offered her money, which she had refused to take. The Inspector makes Mrs Birling admit that the girl believed the money was stolen and so her refusal to accept it was justified. Mrs Birling resists the Inspector's attempts to make her feel sorry for the girl's death. She insists that the blame lies with the girl herself and with the child's father. Sheila fears what may be revealed next and tries to stop her mother from saying any more.

Mrs Birling goes on to show how she believes the child's father is the chief culprit. She says he deserves to be caught and made to publicly admit his guilt. Mrs Birling's arrogant and snobbish self-confidence is not dented by anything Sheila says, and only at the end of the Act does she begin to realise that she may have made a mistake. Her conviction that the father should be made 'an example of' (p. 48) only serves to set a trap for her and for Eric.

Mr Birling is becoming increasingly concerned about the possibility of a public scandal. He is mainly worried because of the effect it could have on his chances of getting a knighthood.

CHECKPOINT 16

In what ways does Eric fit the description of the father of the unborn child?

CHECK THE NET

Priestley's home town of Bradford salutes its famous son on **www.bradford timeline.freeserve.co.uk**

The missing months

The timescale of events leading to the girl's death is brought almost up to date when it is revealed that Mrs Birling saw her only two weeks before. There is still the gap between the end of Gerald's affair with the girl and Mrs Birling's meeting with her.

The girl has used the name Mrs Birling. We later find out why she has done this, but Sheila's increasing agitation, the description of the father and the fact that Eric is the only one who has not yet been questioned are all useful clues as to what might happen next.

Now take a break!

Test yourself (Act II)

Who says ...?

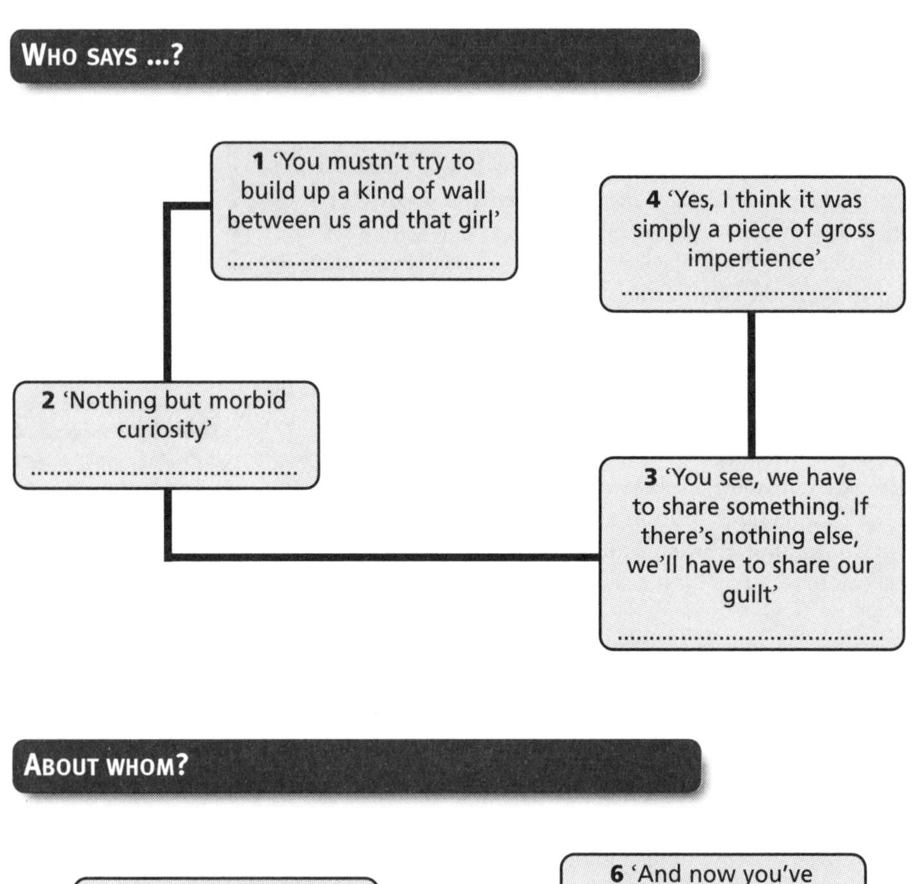

About whom?

5 'It's bound to be unpleasant and disturbing'

....

6 'And now you've made up your mind I must obviously be a selfish, vindictive creature'

....

7 'I rather respect you more than I've ever done before'

....

Check your answers on p. 81.

PART ONE [pp. 50–2] – Eric in the spotlight

1. **Eric realises that they all suspect he had some involvement with the girl.**
2. **Eric admits that he met the girl at the Palace Theatre bar the previous November.**
3. **He starts to tell his story and Mrs Birling is shocked and upset by what he says.**
4. **Mr Birling insists that Sheila takes her mother out to the drawing room.**

When Eric walks in he realises that they all 'know' (p. 50). Sheila tells Eric of his mother's comments and that his heavy drinking has been talked about. Eric is upset, feeling he has been let down. The Inspector now has complete control of the events. His even-handed approach is seen when he overrules Mr Birling and allows Eric to have a drink. Eric tells how he bought the girl drinks and both of them became rather drunk.

EXAMINER'S SECRET

When writing an essay, take care with presentation. Choose your words carefully and avoid slang. A formal essay needs formal language.

Both Eric and Gerald have met the girl at the Palace Theatre bar and both thought she was different from the prostitutes usually found there. Eric's meeting with the girl in November, some two months after Gerald's affair ended, neatly fills in the gap in the girl's history.

Eric explains how he insisted on going with her to where she lived, forced his way in and had sex with her. Eric is careful how he describes what he did, so he simply says 'that's when it happened' (p. 52). Eric's brutish behaviour towards the girl is closely connected with his excessive drinking.

Eric's guilt begins to be made clear. Our earlier suspicions are confirmed and we see the unpleasant nature of his relationship with the girl. Mrs Birling's self-confidence showed signs of cracking at the end of Act II, and Eric's confession starts to make it crumble. She leaves the room.

PART TWO [pp. 52–3] – A baby on the way

CHECKPOINT 17

Pick out some ways in which Gerald's behaviour towards the girl was different from Eric's behaviour towards her.

1. **Eric goes on to detail how he met the girl again two weeks later.**
2. **He describes their meetings and how the girl then told him that she was pregnant.**
3. **He gave her money, but then she refused to accept any more.**
4. **Birling questions his son about where he had obtained the money.**
5. **Eric admits he had taken it from his father's office.**
6. **Sheila and Mrs Birling come back into the room.**

Eric's relationship with the girl is a purely physical one. Eric saw her as so different from the 'fat old tarts' (p. 52) with whom he often saw his father's 'respectable friends' (p. 52). He liked her but he 'wasn't in love with her or anything' (p. 52). He sees her as a 'good sport' (p. 52). She told him a little about herself and he told her his name. They continued to meet but then she told him that she was pregnant. She did not want to marry Eric and he felt that she had treated him like a child.

EXAMINER'S SECRET

Look at the questions carefully. Identify key words and link these to key moments in the action of the play or in the development of the characters.

Details about the girl are vague. Eric does not even mention her name. This uncertainty about her identity is convenient later on in the play when her very existence is questioned.

DID YOU KNOW?

Eric's language in the all-male gathering is coarser than when the ladies are present.

The two Mrs Birlings

Eric has told the girl his name. As he was the father of her child it was natural for her to use his name when applying to the Brumley Women's Charity Organisation for help. That, and her unwillingness to accept stolen money, makes Mrs Birling's refusal to help seem even more petty and unjust.

PART THREE [pp. 53–6] – 'Fire and blood and anguish'

1. **Mr Birling tells his wife that Eric was responsible for the girl's pregnancy and has stolen money from the office.**
2. **Mr Birling begins to plan how he can cover up Eric's fraud.**
3. **Eric is told of Mrs Birling's part in the story and he accuses his mother of killing her own grandchild.**

GLOSSARY

fat old tarts prostitutes

EXAMINER'S SECRET

Read the question carefully. Look for words such as *examine*, *contrast* or *compare* so that you can make an appropriate response.

4. **The Inspector points out how each of them has helped to push the girl towards suicide.**
5. **Before leaving them, the Inspector warns of what will happen if people do not accept that they must live responsibly as part of a caring community.**

Sheila and Mrs Birling return and are told of the latest developments. Eric is surprised that the Inspector already knows that the girl had refused to take the money because it was stolen. When Eric reveals his fraud, Mr Birling is immediately aware of the risk of scandal. Once again his first thoughts are to protect himself and his family's good name. Eric makes it clear that he dared not ask his father for help because he was 'not the kind of father a chap could go to when he's in trouble' (p. 54). When Eric learns of his mother's involvement he becomes increasingly emotional.

The Inspector makes them all listen and he points out to each in turn how they have helped to push the girl towards suicide. He admits that Gerald did at least give the girl some affection and happiness, but stresses that they are all to blame and that they will never forget what they have done. The Inspector's tone becomes prophetic as his final speech foretells what will happen. The Inspector leaves.

The Inspector's repetition of what each has done to harm the girl is a useful reminder of their weaknesses. It shows that the Inspector's job is nearly over, it leaves them to think back on their part in the girl's death and it builds up the sense of guilt before the Inspector's final speech.

As the Inspector leaves there is a noticeable change of mood. Each member of the Birling family is clearly shaken, and their feeling of self-satisfaction has been destroyed.

CHECKPOINT 18

Compare Mr Birling's speeches about a man's responsibility (Act I) with the Inspector's final speech.

The Inspector as Priestley's spokesman

The Inspector's final speech makes a point about responsibility. His references to what will happen in the future make him sound prophetic and suggest he is something more than an ordinary police inspector. It is also used to deliver J.B. Priestley's own strong moral message. Some critics feel he should not have done this, but should have trusted the play to be good enough to carry the message without a sort of sermon being slipped in.

CHECK THE BOOK

Priestley knew about the 'fire and blood and anguish' (p. 56) of war. He describes some of his experiences in his autobiography, *Margin Released*.

PART FOUR [pp. 57–61] – A lesson not learned

1. **The family argue about what has happened.**
2. **Mr Birling is worried that he will not get his knighthood if there is a scandal.**
3. **Sheila is very interested when she learns exactly when the Inspector arrived.**
4. **She wonders if he was a real policeman.**
5. **They believe that if he was not a real policeman then a scandal might be avoided.**
6. **Gerald returns.**

DID YOU KNOW?

An article by Priestley in the November 1957 issue of the magazine the *New Statesman* led to the formation of the Campaign for Nuclear Disarmament, known as CND.

Mr Birling, convinced there will be a public scandal and that he will not receive the hoped-for knighthood, lays the blame on Eric. Eric says he is as ashamed of his parents as they are of him, but Birling still insists that he and his wife were justified in their behaviour. Sheila is angry at her father. She admits her own guilt and is concerned that her parents do not seem to have learnt anything from what has happened during the evening.

Mr Birling clearly feels that Eric is the only one who has behaved in a way which might be seen as directly causing the girl's death. Eric feels that the responsibility is shared equally by them all – Eric's point refers us back to the Inspector's 'chain of events' (Act I, p. 14).

CHECKPOINT 19

How do different characters view the importance of the Inspector's status as a real policeman?

Sheila is struck by the information that the Inspector arrived just as her father had been stating his view that those who believed people were responsible for others were 'cranks' (p. 58). She feels that 'there was something curious about him' and that he 'never seemed like an ordinary police inspector' (p. 59). While she is aware that the Inspector's visit has revealed truths about them, her father and mother are excited by the possibility that he might have been an impostor. Sheila and Eric strongly believe that it makes no difference, but their parents disagree and start to list all the things that seemed odd about him.

You can find information and links to other sites at **www.ontalink.com**

Sheila has faced the truth about herself and her actions rather better than her parents have done. She is amazed and disappointed that there has been no real change in their attitudes. Like Eric, she sees no importance in whether the Inspector was a real policeman or not; for her the important thing is that his visit should make them think about, and accept, their responsibilities.

Keep your attention focused on the question and make sure that everything you write is relevant to that question.

Some people never learn

Birling sees the confessions they have made as rash and weak behaviour. He says they have allowed themselves to be 'bluffed' (p. 60). He can excuse his own admissions since he feels he only sacked the girl for what anyone would accept as good business reasons.

Birling reverts to the ideas that he expressed to Gerald and Eric in Act I, dismissing, as unstable and dangerous political radicals, anyone who expresses humanitarian feelings.

PART FIVE [pp. 61–72] – Three telephone calls

1. **Mr and Mrs Birling keep Sheila from telling Gerald about the involvement of Eric and Mrs Birling.**
2. **Gerald tells them that a local police sergeant has told him that there is no Inspector Goole.**
3. **Mr Birling telephones his friend, the Chief Constable, who confirms their suspicion that there is no Inspector Goole.**
4. **Gerald telephones the Infirmary, and learns that no-one has been taken there after drinking disinfectant.**
5. **Gerald tries to persuade Sheila to take back the ring, but she feels she needs time to think.**
6. **The telephone rings, and when Birling answers it he is told that a police inspector is on his way to the house to make enquiries about a young girl's suicide.**

EXAMINER'S SECRET

Always allow yourself some time to check your work. If you are working at home, read your essay out aloud; if in an exam, mouth the words as you read silently and slowly.

Gerald questions whether the photographs might have been of different girls and even wonders whether the story of a girl committing suicide wasn't simply used to shock them into making damaging admissions. Sheila and Eric do not join in the celebrations. They cannot forget what has happened.

CHECKPOINT 20

How do their reactions make Sheila and Eric different from the others?

It is Gerald who first brings some proof that the Inspector was not a member of the local police force. They have all behaved cruelly towards a girl, but, prompted by Gerald's news, they come to think that it might not have been the same girl. Gerald uses the uncertainty about the girl's name, and the fact that no-one else saw the photograph shown to any one character, to suggest that there might have been several different girls – one girl that Mr Birling sacked from his factory, one girl that Sheila had had sacked from Milwards, one that Gerald had an affair with and one who was made pregnant by Eric and who probably tried to get help from Mrs Birling. This leads him to questioning whether there is a dead girl at all. Birling is greatly relieved when the Infirmary has no record of any suicide, and Mrs Birling congratulates Gerald on how he has 'argued this very cleverly' (p. 70).

Mr and Mrs Birling join Gerald in eagerly trying to improve their own situation by discrediting the Inspector. Emphasis is placed on the idea that it has all been a trick, 'a lot of moonshine. Nothing but an elaborate sell!' (p. 70), so reducing the seriousness of the admissions they have all made.

Eric and Sheila do not share the relief felt by the others. They have been so deeply affected by the evening's events that the truth of the Inspector's identity makes no difference to them. These two know that things can never be quite as they were before and they have learnt something which will change the way they behave in the future. They cannot forget what they have done.

As Mr Birling tries to make a joke out of what has happened, the telephone rings. He answers and hears that a police inspector is on his way ...

DID YOU KNOW?

J.B. Priestley wrote novels as well as about fifty plays. He also founded his own production company and was the director of the Mask Theatre in London.

A piece of pure theatre

The telephone call at the end reopens the question of the Inspector's identity. It also leaves the audience wondering whether it will be the same Inspector who comes to question them and how events will progress this time round. The final telephone call was described by Stephen Potter as 'the best *coup de theatre* of the year'.

GLOSSARY

moonshine nonsense
an elaborate sell a complicated confidence trick

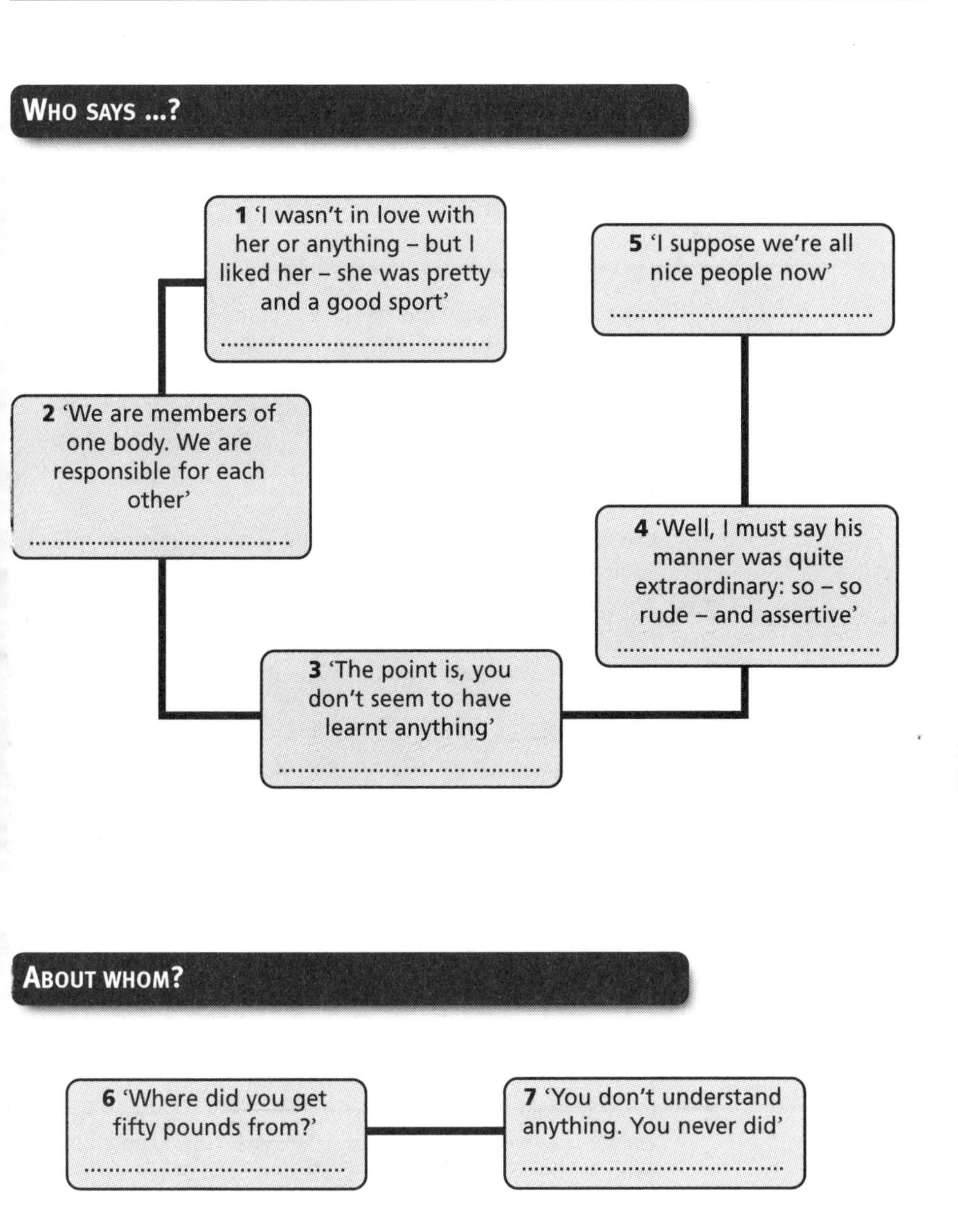

Check your answers on p. 81.

COMMENTARY

EXAMINER'S SECRET

Answer the question that has been set – not one you wished had been set!

THEMES

SOCIAL MESSAGE

In this play, J.B. Priestley presents us with a sincerely felt and powerfully expressed social message:

- We are shown the comfortable home and rich way of life of the Birling family.
- By contrast we have the accounts of the desperate attempts of the workers to increase their poor wages and the drab and sordid life that the girl is forced to live as a result of the actions of people such as the Birlings.
- The Inspector champions the cause of the poor.
- He tries to get the others to accept that all people share a common humanity and so are all part of an interdependent community.

This message does seem to get through to Sheila and Eric. Sheila is ready to accept and demonstrate this feeling of compassion, but her father simply dismisses the idea of a community, in which responsibility and guilt are shared, as the foolish mutterings of a socialist crank.

MORALITY

As the play progresses, the Inspector's point is put across more and more forcefully.

- Each character's involvement with Eva Smith/Daisy Renton adds to the Inspector's argument.
- He becomes not only a spokesman for the disadvantaged but a voice for the conscience which the Birlings and Gerald seem to lack!
- The characters, especially the older ones, are increasingly shown to be hiding behind an appearance of respectability which has no foundation in any true sense of morality.

The Inspector points out what would happen if injustice and inequality were allowed to continue unchecked. His increasingly missionary tone reaches its peak when J.B. Priestley's political message is thundered out in the Inspector's final speech. This exaggerated oratorical style (**hyperbole**) might not be acceptable if J.B. Priestley had not gradually built up the mysterious and prophetic aspects of the Inspector's character.

Political view

We are never given a clear set of political policies but J.B. Priestley does make the general point that all of us have a share in the responsibility for what happens in our society, that we have a duty of care to others:

- We see that the sense of respectability with which the characters surround themselves does not stand up to close examination.
- The way that the older characters remain unmoved and immovable, uncaring for anyone but themselves, is one of the horrors of the play.
- Each of the revelations deepens the lesson they should be learning but they refuse to take any notice.

We are left wondering whether our society today is any more likely to survive a similarly close examination. Are we any better in our everyday dealings with other people than the Birlings?

Responsibility

Most of the characters have a narrow view of what it means to be responsible, but the Inspector provides us with a much broader one:

- MR BIRLING is a businessman and as such he feels his responsibility is to make a success of his business. This means making as much profit as possible, even if that means being harsh in his dealings with those who work for him.

  As a family man he sees that he has a responsibility to provide for the material needs of his family, yet it is clear that Eric does not see him as the kind of father to whom he could turn when in trouble.

CHECK THE NET

There is some useful general information on J.B. Priestley to be found on **www.miskatonic.org**

EXAMINER'S SECRET

Try producing a single revision sheet for each of the key characters and themes. Set it out in the form of a diagram with essential quotations and some **phrases of your own**.

- MRS BIRLING accepts her responsibility as chairwoman of the Women's Charity Organisation, but only sees a responsibility to help those that she feels are deserving of help.
- SHEILA belatedly recognises that as a powerful customer she has an obligation not to let her personal feelings and ill-temper lead to misery for people who have no power.

Remember that characters are revealed through what others say about them as well as what they themselves say and do

- ERIC has little sense of responsibility. He drinks far more than is good for him and he forced the girl into a relationship which had disastrous consequences. He attempted to help her by stealing from his father.
- GERALD showed some sense of responsibility when he rescued the girl from the unwelcome attentions of another man, fed her and found her somewhere to live. Yet he gave in to his own desire for personal pleasure and eventually abandoned the girl without knowing, or very much caring, what happened to her.

The Inspector's role is to shake these people up and to make them aware of that broader view of responsibility which J.B. Priestley felt was essential if the world was ever going to learn from its mistakes and become a place where everyone has the right to be treated fairly.

LOVE

The play presents a variety of thoughts about love, the nature of love and different people's interpretation of love:

- Sheila and Gerald appear to be in love; they have just announced their engagement and seem happy enough contemplating a future dedicated to each other.
- After each of them has confessed to their shameful behaviour towards Eva Smith/Daisy Renton, Sheila realises that they do not really know each other well and that trust is an essential ingredient in a loving relationship.
- Mr Birling's remark about the engagement of his daughter bringing the two family firms into a closer working relationship, gives us an indication of his attitude towards love and marriage. He sees marriage as a convenient way of progressing up the social and economic ladder. This makes us wonder whether love played

any real part in his marriage to the socially superior Sybil Birling and whether her coldness to others, including her own children, does not have its roots in a loveless marriage.

- Both Gerald and Eric have been involved with the girl, yet each of them denies that they loved her – their relationships were prompted by physical attraction.
- The girl took up with Eric out of necessity, but she does, however, seem to have felt a genuine love for Gerald. Gerald's ending of the affair may be seen as being callous in view of her love for him.

The Inspector preaches a form of love, not too dissimilar to that preached by Christ when he instructed his followers to love one another as much as they love themselves. This form of love is the true 'charity', and is something which appears quite alien to women such as Mrs Birling who bask in the glory of volunteering their time to 'charity' while being devoid of any true charity in their hearts.

CHECK THE BOOK

Charles Dickens in *A Christmas Carol* shows the miser Scrooge given the opportunity both to look back on his past life and forward to the future so that he is able to change his ways and so avoid the tragic consequences of his meanness.

TIME

J.B. Priestley wrote the play for an audience just coming out of the horrors of the Second World War, yet he set his play in 1912, two years before the start of the First World War and this brings us to a consideration of J.B. Priestley's use of time as an element of his plays. At the end of the play we are left with a sense that the events are going to start all over again. We wonder whether things will be different and how the characters will behave.

Ouspensky's theory

J.B. Priestley became fascinated by theories about the nature of time. Put simply, most of us see time as a straight line going from one point to another in a continuous sequence. J.B. Priestley read P.D. Ouspensky's book *A New Model of the Universe* in which it was suggested that when we die we re-enter our life once more from the beginning. We are born again in the same house to the same parents and continue to repeat all the events of our life just as before. This cycle of identical lives would go on being repeated if we changed nothing of significance. If, however, we improved in some spiritual way, we could convert the circle into a spiral of events that would, if

CHECK THE BOOK

If you wanted to explore J.B. Priestley's time theories in greater detail, you might also like to read his plays *I Have Been Here Before* and *Time and the Conways*. His plays are regularly included in the programmes of local theatre companies and are well worth a visit.

we continued to make significant improvements, eventually open the way for us to escape from the repetitions and into a new life in which we did not repeat our mistakes.

Dunne's theory

J.W. Dunne was another time theorist who influenced J.B. Priestley. Dunne laid out the idea that you could be given the gift of seeing forward in time as well as looking back. This would mean that, just as you can look back and see what actions led to your present situation, you could look forward and see the consequences of your actions. So, if you wished, you could change those actions and so avoid the consequences.

CHECK THE FILM

Modern films, such as *Back to the Future*, use the idea of intervention by a superior being to bring about a change to the lives of others by affecting what has happened in the past; while *Groundhog Day* uses the notion of time being circular, though it is condensed into a repetition of one day rather than a repetition of lifetimes!

An Inspector Calls contains elements of these time theories:

- The Inspector, arriving before the suicide is a reality, offers each character a chance to see the consequences, to change the future, to break the circle. Eric and Sheila seem prepared to take that opportunity to face up to their past actions and to improve themselves, but the others do not.
- The reflections on the past, and the possibilities of the future highlight the importance of caring for others, of taking responsibility for our actions and of considering the consequences of them.
- The Inspector's knowledge of events, apparently before they happen, his steady revelation of the characters' pasts and their links to the dead girl over a two-year period gives him a mystical, unworldly quality – what J.C. Trewin in his review of the play in the *Observer* in 1946 called 'the angel with the flaming sword'.
- The Inspector's departure leaves the characters free to decide their future, while at the end we are left to wonder how they will cope with reliving the close scrutiny of their dealings with others when the cycle starts all over again.

By setting the play in 1912 and presenting it to a later audience, J.B. Priestley has covered an era which includes both World Wars. The failure of the older characters to learn anything reflects the failure of generations to learn from the mistakes of the recent past. There is **dramatic irony** in that characters talk of hopes for peace and prosperity, but we know these will not happen. By 1945 J.B. Priestley was hoping that the second time around the world might learn from past mistakes and we might see such hopes realised if we, the audience, can accept the challenge to be caring and socially aware.

CHECK THE BOOK

If you want to find out more about the life and times of J.B. Priestley himself, you might like to read Vincent Brome's biography *J.B. Priestley*, especially the section dealing with the 'time plays'.

STRUCTURE

This play follows the tradition of what is known as a **well-made play**. It has a plot in which the action flows smoothly and all the parts fit together precisely, rather like parts of a jigsaw puzzle. As a result the characters and the audience move from a state of ignorance to a state of knowledge. J.B. Priestley wanted his play to have a uniformity of manner and tone with one situation rapidly moving on to the next. He felt that he could best achieve this by writing quickly, and indeed he completed this play in a week. **The unities** of time and place is achieved by the events all taking place in the dining room and the action running continuously through all the three Acts. Even when there is a break between Acts where an interval might be placed, the start of the next Act takes us to the same point in time at which we left the action.

The action is taken forward by the Inspector's questioning of each character in turn. Their reasons for entering or leaving are always plausible and always allow some new aspect of the plot to be introduced or something mentioned earlier to be developed. The play is built up in a series of episodes and each character has either a leading or supporting role in each of these episodes, even in their absence. Gerald's decision to go for a walk, for example, means that he can alter the course of events after the Inspector's departure, while Eric's similar absence allows his involvement with Eva Smith/Daisy Renton to be explored in a way that it could not be if he were present. Each new revelation, prompted by the Inspector's careful use of the photograph or information from the diary, adds to the overall picture of those two crucial years in the girl's life. Each part fits together and helps to complete the jigsaw of events and involvements.

EXAMINER'S SECRET

When writing about a specific scene or extract always make connections with the play as a whole – this at least shows you have read the complete work!

As the pattern develops, the audience is able to predict what will happen next.

EXAMINER'S SECRET

A feature of 'A'-grade writing on literature is the ability to see two possibilities of interpretations and to support a preference for one of them.

J.B. Priestley brings about quite subtle changes of mood. The play begins in a mood of high celebration, but after the Inspector's entrance, the other characters have little reason for self-congratulation and the mood becomes more sombre, even threatening. By the time the Inspector delivers his final speech the mood has become one that promises real danger for the future. The relief that is felt when the Inspector is seemingly shown up as a hoaxer and no evidence of a suicide can be found is shattered by the dramatic telephone call. J.B. Priestley even uses **stage directions** to suggest how the lighting effects can reflect the mood. He orders a '*pink and intimate*' (p. 1) use of lights for the party which changes to '*brighter and harder*' (p. 1) when the Inspector's investigation begins.

Although the action and the time span of the play is realistic, J.B. Priestley throws in two twists at the end. Firstly we have the problem of who the Inspector really was: a trickster determined to make fools of them or some sort of avenging spirit come to make them see the evil of their ways? The second twist is the time-release mechanism when the telephone call interrupts and takes them back to relive the events. It is this which allows the possibility that the Inspector was a real policeman who has slipped out of real time and will return. If they fail to learn from their experiences and are 'ready to go on in the same old way' (Act III, p. 71) the Inspector's threat of 'fire and blood and anguish' (Act III, p. 56) will become their reality.

CHARACTERS

THE INSPECTOR

EXAMINER'S SECRET

It is always a good idea to collect a range of words to describe a character.

The word 'inspector' suggests someone who looks closely at things, and this is his role in the events of the play. The name 'Goole' is the same as the seaport town of Goole at the mouth of the River Humber, and perhaps suggests that the Inspector is going to fish for information, to trawl through the lives and deeply hidden secrets of the other characters. The name also sounds like ghoul – someone with a morbid interest in death, a spirit which is said to take fresh life from corpses, and it is certainly arguable that the Inspector's existence is a result of the girl's death.

Mysterious
Imposing
Sombre
Determined
Calm

Described as creating '*an impression of massiveness, solidity and purposefulness*' (Act I, p. 11), the Inspector grows as the stories of each character are revealed. He remains solid and intact as each of them breaks down, and nothing the others can do or say distracts him from his purpose.

He arrives just after Mr Birling has been setting out his view of life: that every man must only look out for himself. The Inspector's role is to show that this is not the case. Throughout the play he demonstrates how people are responsible for how they affect the lives of others and his views are summed up in his visionary and dramatic final speech. It is the Inspector who makes things happen. Without him none of the secrets would ever have come into the open. He seems to know what each character has done, and his probing questions leave them to confess in their own way. From the moment of his arrival he seems different. His sombre appearance and the news he brings are a contrast with the happy and elegant air of celebration. Despite the importance in the local community of people like Gerald and the Birlings, he controls the development of events: who will speak and when; who may or may not leave; who will or will not see the photograph. He even seems to control what people say. Sheila, who has commented on his mysterious character, tells Gerald 'Somehow he makes you' (Act II, p. 37). The Inspector has Eva Smith's diary and a letter. From these he has built up a picture of her life and character. He uses this information, with constant reminders of the horrific death she has suffered, to force them to face up to what they have done. He links the series of wrongs done to the girl so that they are seen to build up to pressure which forces her to her last desperate act.

The way he uses the information he has creates an impression of someone who is both an outsider and an all-knowing creature. This makes him appear mysterious and powerful. Yet J.B. Priestley can only use him as a catalyst, as someone who creates the possibility for others to face up to what they have done. They must decide for themselves whether to change or not. He is a character who represents J.B. Priestley's strong moral view. His comments show a compassion which extends to those who recognise the wrong they have done. He does not forgive what they have done, but when they freely admit their faults he allows them to see that they can find forgiveness through future good behaviour. This moral dimension makes him different from an ordinary policeman. He is more concerned with right and wrong than with what is or is not legal. His lack of fear or favour, his determined questioning and control of events may be what is expected of a policeman, but towards the end of the play it is those same qualities (identified by Mrs Birling as rudeness) which fuel suspicions about him. His approach has been perhaps too abrasive, and he is clearly someone for whom social conventions count for nothing when weighed against the desire for truth and justice.

MR BIRLING

Wealthy businessman
Involved in local politics
Pompous
Unsophisticated
Bully

Mr Birling is a successful businessman who has been active in local politics and has had the honour of being Lord Mayor. He is a magistrate and has hopes of being given a knighthood which will make him socially closer to Sir George and Lady Croft. He is described as a '*heavy-looking rather portentous man*' (Act I, p. 1). His size perhaps helps to give him the threatening appearance suggested by that description. He is self-confident, but his upbringing makes him less socially aware and gracious than either his wife or Gerald Croft. He sees the engagement of Gerald and Sheila as being good for business and later it is business interests which most affect his attitude to Eric's theft of money from the firm.

His view of his own importance leads him:

- To try to use his social status to intimidate the Inspector
- To try to impose his will and authority on Eric and Sheila
- To be concerned about the effect of a scandal on his chances of a knighthood

It is central to the play that his attitude that 'a man has to mind his own business and look after his own' (Act I, p. 10) is discredited by the confessions that the Inspector draws out. Yet he does not change his views or attitudes over the course of the play. Though he reveals more of his contempt for weakness and his anger at the foolish behaviour of others, he cannot see that his actions towards the girl were wrong, and we feel that if the events were repeated, he would still feel justified in sacking the girl. He feels this was, and still is, the right attitude for a man of business. He sees nothing strange in wanting to protect Sheila from the unpleasantness of the girl's life and death, yet feels no guilt at not having protected the girl herself.

After the Inspector has gone he simply wants things to return to the way they were. He cannot understand Sheila's and Eric's insistence that there is something to be learnt, and he is relieved and triumphant when he feels that scandal has been avoided and everything is all right. Despite his self-centred and unrepentant attitude it is possible to feel some sympathy for him at the end of the play when his relief that the incident is over and done with is shattered by the telephone call. Perhaps we can feel this because J.B. Priestley lets us see someone who is so blindly wrong and never as in control of events as he would like himself, and others, to think.

MRS BIRLING

Mrs Birling is described as a '*rather cold woman and her husband's social superior*' (Act I, p. 1). Her coldness and lack of conscience make her unsympathetic, while her keen awareness of the rules of polite behaviour (shown, for example, in the way she rebukes her husband for his comment about the quality of the meal) makes her seem out of touch with what really matters. Her lack of understanding of how other people live is shown in her snobbish comments about 'a girl of that sort' (Act II, p. 47) and in her unwillingness to believe the girl's reasons for refusing to take the stolen money or marry the foolish young man responsible for her pregnancy. Her lack of understanding even extends to her family as she has been quite unaware of her own son's heavy drinking.

Cold
Unfeeling
Socially correct
Self-important
Out-of-touch with reality of life

She remains untouched by the Inspector's questioning, and refuses to see how her actions could have been responsible for the girl's death. We can clearly see that her refusal to help the girl could easily have been what finally led to her suicide, yet it is only when she realises that Eric was the child's father and so her actions have resulted in the

EXAMINER'S SECRET

There is no need to always provide lengthy quotations. Key words like 'excited' taken from the text can be more effective.

death of her own grandchild that she begins to show any signs of weakening. The speed with which she recovers after the Inspector's departure emphasises how cold and unsympathetic a character she is.

She can be seen as hypocritical because:

- She claims to be shocked by Eric's drinking and the talk of immoral relationships with the girl, yet she cannot bear not to hear Eric's confession.
- She is quite content to lay all the blame on the father of the child. When it becomes clear that the young man is her son, she is not prepared to own up to her comments until Sheila brings them into the open.
- Early on she condemns Gerald's 'disgusting affair' (Act II, p. 38) but seems quite willing to forget about it once the threat of shared blame seems to have been withdrawn.

There is no sense of relief that her selfish actions have not been the cause of tragedy. The glowing thanks and praise that she lavishes on Gerald for the clever way he appears to have settled things reflect her desire to remain untouched by outside events and to maintain the appearance of respectability.

SHEILA BIRLING

Sheila is described as '*a pretty girl in her early twenties, very pleased with life and rather excited*' (Act I, pp. 1–2). Early on in the play she is playful and rather self-centred, enjoying the attention and importance that her engagement is bringing her. Her curiosity when she finds her father, Eric and Gerald with the Inspector is at first superficial, but she soon shows a sensitive side to her nature and is moved by the news of the girl's death. Her own happiness seems almost unfair to her and, even before she has any idea of her own part in the dead girl's story, she seems truly interested. Unlike her father, she responds to the girl as a person, not as cheap labour. She is prepared to criticise her father and shows that though she is foolish and selfish, she has the potential to change.

When Sheila realises that her own jealousy and bad temper have led to the girl losing her job at the shop, she is genuinely sorry. Yet we also see that her sorrow is linked to her feeling of regret that she will not be able to go back to a favourite shop, and so her streak of selfishness is still there. By the end of Act I, Sheila is already aware of the influence of the Inspector and is beginning to question how deep his knowledge goes. She warns Gerald 'Of course he knows. And I hate to think how much he knows that we don't know yet' (Act I, p. 26).

Young
Pretty
Lively
Selfish
Ill-tempered
Later sympathetic, repentant and caring

Sheila grows stronger and more sympathetic as the play goes on. She is obviously upset by Gerald's confession, but is strong enough to cope with it and even to acknowledge that she is impressed by Gerald's honesty. Her realisation that honesty and truth really matter shows that she is capable of learning and changing. She has begun to have some understanding of what the Inspector is doing so that she is able to see the world, and her responsibility, according to his values instead of those of her family. This is why she can see the trap her mother's arrogance is creating, and why she tries to stop her mother from exposing and condemning the child's father. It is only Sheila and Eric, the two youngest and 'more impressionable' (Act II, p. 30) characters who feel everyone needs to learn something from what has happened. Sheila does seem to have learnt something and to have changed, and we feel that her future attitude to others will be more caring, self-controlled and responsible.

ERIC BIRLING

Unlike his sister, Sheila, Eric is awkward: '*not quite at ease, half shy, half assertive*' (Act I, p. 2). He does not seem to have his father's affection or approval. He is kept out of the information about his father's possible knighthood, and when he really needed help he felt his father was 'not the kind of father a chap could go to when he's in trouble' (Act III, p. 54). He drinks too much, has forced his way into the girl's home, has made the girl pregnant and stolen money.

Like Sheila, he feels sympathy for Eva Smith as soon as he hears how Mr Birling sacked her. When he has to admit how he behaved towards her he has a stronger sense of guilt than the others because the consequences of what he did are so much worse. It is not

Awkward
Immature
Thoughtless
Selfish
Drunkard
Thief

surprising that he turns violently on his mother when he learns how she refused to help the girl. He curses his mother and accuses her of killing both the girl and the child. He has been rude to his father earlier and his rudeness to his parents increases the more he drinks. One can imagine how frightening he might have seemed to the girl when he was drunk – 'in that state when a chap easily turns nasty' (Act III, p. 52). His immaturity shows in his casual attitude towards his relationship with the girl whom he regarded as a 'good sport' (Act III, p. 52) although she treated him like a child. He appears to have learnt very little from his privileged education.

Yet he is one of the young ones who has been impressed by the Inspector. He wants his parents to admit their mistakes as freely as he has admitted his. Though he is not a particularly pleasant character, we may feel that he has learnt a lesson, that he is sincerely ashamed of his behaviour and that he is capable of changing for the better.

GERALD CROFT

Self-assured
Well mannered
Business man
Sense of chivalry but is morally weak

Gerald is the son of Birling's rival industrialist, Sir George Croft. He has the self-confidence of someone who is at ease wherever he is or whoever he is with. He is polite and tactful with Mr and Mrs Birling. Being about thirty, he is older than Sheila and Eric, whose parents treat Gerald as something of an equal. He is trusted with the secret of Arthur Birling's possible knighthood. Gerald's views on the way a business should be run, how workers should be treated and the importance of profit are all in line with those of Mr Birling, and he supports the reasoning with which Mr Birling justifies Eva Smith's sacking from the firm.

When he first met Daisy Renton he saved her from the awkward situation with Alderman Meggarty and set out to help her. His good intentions, however, went astray. He found Daisy attractive from the start, and he allowed his feelings to develop. He felt affection for her but admits that her feelings for him were stronger than his feelings for her. He felt guilty about only being able to offer her temporary help and when he left her he gave her money to help her to start a new life. The fact that he 'made her happy for a time' (Act III, p. 56) allows us to feel some sympathy for him. His regret for the way he used her is genuine, but he does not have the same deep response as

Sheila to the Inspector's message. He acts on his suspicions, and as a result he is the one who begins the chain of events leading to the feeling of certainty that Goole was an impostor.

EDNA

Edna, the maid, appears only briefly. Her presence strengthens the impression of the solidity, privilege and wealth which the Birlings enjoy. It is Edna, the only one of the working people in the household that we see on stage, who announces the Inspector's arrival.

EVA SMITH/DAISY RENTON

The girl remains a mystery. She never appears on stage and we do not know her real name, but the play revolves round the last two years of her life. We know she was pretty enough to make Sheila jealous and to have attracted the attention of both Gerald and Eric. What we learn about her, her drab life and unpleasant death, contrasts sharply with what we see and learn of the Birling family and Gerald Croft. She worked hard, supported her fellow workers and was kind and gentle. Although she was reduced to earning her living by picking up men in the Palace Theatre bar, she did not seem well suited to that way of life. Her sense of right and wrong prevented her from considering marriage to Eric and protected him from his folly in stealing money from his father's firm. Despite five separate stories, she remains more of a symbol than a real person. She stands for all the people we meet in our everyday lives. J.B. Priestley uses her tragedy to jolt us into thinking about our responsibility towards others. She is the weapon the Inspector uses to try to change the attitudes of the others. His final speech reminds us that 'One Eva Smith has gone – but there are millions and millions and millions of Eva Smiths and John Smiths still left with us, with their lives, their hopes and fears, their suffering and chance of happiness, all intertwined with our lives, and what we think and say and do' (Act III, p. 56).

A good answer will show that you can interpret and analyse points in the text, so avoid vague general statements.

Now take a break!

LANGUAGE AND STYLE

THE REALISM OF PRIESTLEY'S LANGUAGE

Plays are meant to be performed, and the language of a play suggests the action which should be taking place. When reading a play we can see the way that the words also suggest a mood, and there are times when they help to group characters together, placing individuals in opposing groups to other characters. The Inspector's passionate and heartfelt words as he prepares to leave (Act III p. 6) are reflected by the passion Sheila shows as she struggles against her parents' complacent refusal to accept that anything has changed. The language also reveals character, and there are times when what the character says is in conflict with what the character does. Many of the characters reflect the hypocrisy which Priestley was condemning.

The play has elements of the Medieval **morality play** since it shows characters who are guilty of one or more of the Seven Deadly Sins, and through the Inspector Priestley hopes to point his moral out to us. The Inspector, and later Sheila, becomes the mouthpiece for Priestley's ideas. When a writer uses his work in this way, he is being **didactic** or producing a polemical piece of writing. The play conforms to the three **unities** of the **well-made play**. This means that the action is focused on one story-line, that there is only one setting, and that the time of action on stage is identical to the real time that the action takes. Priestley uses the conventions of the well-made play to build up the sense of mystery and suspense. The first scene gently introduces us to the main characters, and from then on each entrance or exit highlights a dramatic moment. Several scenes in turn reveal secrets and the end of each Act builds to a tense and climactic moment. The play also, of course, has elements of a **'whodunnit'** since the girl's story is gradually revealed through the Inspector's careful questioning of the 'suspects'. The Inspector's final speech has all the dramatic power of any scene in which a detective strips away the layers of evidence to reveal the guilty party, but Priestley then produces further twists and turns leading to the final telephone call which leaves us guessing once again.

EXAMINER'S SECRET

If you can take your own annotated copy of a text into the exam, be sure that your notes comply with the exam board's regulations.

The realism of the play, its realistic set and realistic incidents, is reinforced by the realism of the language. There is a clear, no-

nonsense approach to the **dialogue** but because the speech is so grammatically correct it does not reflect the true patterns of everyday speech in a way that a modern play by Harold Pinter or Dennis Potter would. The realism of language is, however, the realism of 1912, and though the language of Edwardian England differs in some respects to what sounds natural today, there are no real problems of communication.

There is an emphasis on correct behaviour and good manners – especially in Mrs Birling's speeches – yet the Inspector frequently interrupts characters who are not going in the direction he wishes them to go in. The interruptions balance the often lively dialogues and **monologues** which carry the story-line forward, but the Inspector's interruptions and his indifference to the nicer points of polite behaviour make him stand apart from the others every bit as much as does his precise and incisive language.

EXAMINER'S SECRET

An 'A' student is able to provide a detailed account of language features, or structured patterns, to support a conclusion about the author's intentions.

We are told that the Inspector speaks '*carefully, weightily*' (Act I, p. 10) and we can see that what he says consists largely of questions and instructions. This helps him to control, direct and develop the plot. Language helps to reinforce the Inspector's authority. His words are often matter-of-fact, as we would expect from a policeman, but the tone is commanding and even threatening. His final speech uses a quite different sort of language: it is the language of the prophet or the missionary and sounds more like a sermon than the carefully weighed evidence of a policeman. There are times when he produces dramatic results by use of a very short and isolated sentence – or even a single word. At other times he speaks in long sentences which are broken up to produce a rhythm which gives what he says extra emphasis and makes what he says profoundly logical, e.g. 'Because what happened to her then may have determined what happened to her afterwards, and what happened to her afterwards may have driven her to suicide' (Act I, p. 14). Those words are followed by the terse comment 'A chain of events' (Act I, p. 14) and we can see that the logical sequence links up just like the links of the chain.

The language used by each character helps us to create a clearer picture of them:

- MR BIRLING, we are told, is *'rather provincial in his speech'* (Act I, p. 1) and he frequently speaks in a rather bullying and forceful manner which at times mirrors what he felt was expected of a solid, middle-class Edwardian without being really convincing. His comments about a possible knighthood and his congratulations to the cook are not in keeping with correct behaviour, but they do seem to reflect Birling's arrogant and pompous nature.

EXAMINER'S SECRET

When you have identified a literary term, you should comment on its effectiveness.

- GERALD CROFT, however, is inevitably careful and correct in what he says. For example, cleverly freeing Mr Birling from his social error about the good meal by his careful comment about being one of the family, and later using a **euphemism** instead of saying 'prostitute'. His one lapse is in his description of Alderman Meggarty, and that may reflect the anger he felt as a result of his care for Daisy Renton.
- SHEILA AND ERIC are less restrained and their use of slang expressions such as 'squiffy' (Act I, p. 3) shock their parents and show up the generation gap as clearly as do their bitter comments on their parents' behaviour.

IMAGERY

Sheila can become quite emotional, as she does when describing the events in Milwards or when she is warning her mother not to try 'to build up a kind of wall' (Act II, p. 30) between the family and the girl. This is one of the most powerful images in the play, yet the Inspector also uses powerful images. Many of the images he conjures up are hard-hitting and create strong dramatic effects. In Act I he talks about how the disinfectant has 'burnt her inside out' (Act I, p. 11), and he recalls the same image in Act II when he tries to shock Mrs Birling by telling her that the girl's position is 'that she lies with a burnt-out inside on a slab' (Act II, p. 46). Throughout the play the Inspector uses phrases such as 'great agony' (Act I, p. 11), 'died, after several hours of agony' (Act I, p. 17) and 'died in misery and agony' (Act I, p. 28) as well as repeating short, sharp, almost brutal reminders that the girl is dead. By doing this, Priestley keeps the picture of the girl in the mortuary constantly before our eyes.

IRONY

Priestley also makes use of **irony** and **sarcasm**. Sheila is sarcastic in saying that she had not thought Gerald meant Buckingham Palace when he had said that he met the girl in the stalls bar 'at the Palace' (Act II, p. 34). Gerald's response: 'Thanks. You're going to be a great help, I can see' (Act II, p. 34) is clearly ironic. This is quickly followed by Sheila's reference to Gerald as the 'hero' (Act II, p. 34) of the story he is telling and Gerald's reply that he is glad he is amusing her. A little later, when Gerald tells the Inspector that Daisy Renton accepted the end of the affair rather better than he had expected, Sheila retorts 'That was nice for you' (Act II, p. 38). By this comment she shows how hurt she is and how unpleasant his story has been for her.

Some examination questions have prompts to help you. Don't ignore them but use them as a starting point for planning your answer.

The Inspector is even more ironic in one of his early exchanges with Mr Birling in Act I. Birling claims that it would be 'very awkward' if we had to be 'responsible for everything that happened to everybody we'd had anything to do with' (Act I, p. 14). The Inspector echoes Birling's words 'Very awkward' (Act I, p. 14). At first we might think that the Inspector was agreeing with Birling, but we come to realise that he is hinting that what is to follow is indeed going to become very awkward because he will show that they are responsible, and will be held to be responsible, for what they have done to the girl.

Much of the play's success depends upon the **dramatic irony** which J.B. Priestley creates. We see this in the mistaken view that Mr Birling has about the future, his faith in technology and belief in peace. We can guess from this that his view of a man's responsibility will be equally wrong. Similarly, when Sheila has worked out that Eric might well be the father of Eva Smith's child, there is irony in that Mrs Birling has not realised it and is unwittingly demanding that an example should be made of none other than her own son.

Perhaps there is a different sort of irony in the fact that the Inspector has been talking as much to us, the audience, as to the characters. We have to ask ourselves whether we are in a position to judge what has happened when we are probably as guilty of acting irresponsibly and unkindly as anyone on stage! This irony strengthens our feeling that J.B. Priestley's type of socialism is not so much about politics but about caring and even, perhaps, about love.

RESOURCES

EXAMINER'S SECRET

In a typical examination you might use as many as eight quotations.

HOW TO USE QUOTATIONS

One of the secrets of success in writing essays is the way you use quotations. There are five basic principles:

1. Put inverted commas at the beginning and end of the quotation.
2. Write the quotation exactly as it appears in the original.
3. Do not use a quotation that repeats what you have just written.
4. Use the quotation so that it fits into your sentence.
5. Keep the quotation as short as possible.

Quotations should be used to develop the line of thought in your essays. Your comment should not duplicate what is in your quotation. For example:

> **Gerald Croft tells the Inspector that he first met Daisy Renton in the bar of the local theatre the previous spring, 'I met her first, sometime in March last year, in the stalls bar at the Palace' (Act II, p. 34).**

Far more effective is to write:

> **Gerald Croft says that he first met Daisy Renton 'in the stalls bar at the Palace' (Act II, p. 34).which is the local music hall theatre.**

Always lay out the lines as they appear in the text. For example:

> **The revelation leads Eric to turn savagely on his mother:**
>
> **'... yes, and you killed her – and the child she'd have had too – my child – your own grandchild – you killed them both – damn you, damn you –' (Act III, p. 55).**

However, the most sophisticated way of using the writer's words is to embed them into your sentence:

Gerald, seeing that Alderman Meggarty was 'half-drunk and goggle-eyed' (Act II, p. 35), wanted to rescue Daisy Renton from him.

When you use quotations in this way, you are demonstating the ability to use text as evidence to support your ideas – not simply including words from the original to prove you have read it.

COURSEWORK ESSAY

Set aside an hour or so at the start of your work to plan what you have to do.

- List all the points you feel are needed to cover the task. Collect page references of information and quotations that will support what you have to say. A helpful tool is the highlighter pen: this saves painstaking copying and enables you to target precisely what you want to use.
- Focus on what you consider to be the main points of the essay. Try to sum up your argument in a single sentence, which could be the closing sentence of your essay. Depending on the essay title, it could be a statement about a character: Sheila Birling is one of the more sensitive characters in *An Inspector Calls*, as she clearly becomes fully aware of her responsibility and, despite her parents, she is prepared to change her selfish ways; an opinion about setting: I believe that the heavy comfort of the Birling family's dining room accurately reflects that family's comfortable sense of contentment with life; or a judgement on a theme: I think that the main theme of *An Inspector Calls* is responsibility, because the Inspector's questioning reveals the irresponsible behaviour of each of the other characters in turn.
- Make a short essay plan. Use the first paragraph to introduce the argument you wish to make. In the following paragraphs develop this argument with details, examples and other possible points of view. Sum up your argument in the last paragraph. Check you have answered the question.
- Write the essay, remembering all the time the central point you are making.

An 'A'-grade candidate can analyse a variety of the writer's techniques.

- On completion, go back over what you have written to eliminate careless errors and improve expression. Read it aloud to yourself, or, if you are feeling more confident, to relative or friend.

If you can, try to type you essay, using a word processor. This will allow you to correct and improve your writing without spoiling its appearance.

SITTING THE EXAMINATION

Examination papers are carefully designed to give you the opportunity to do your best. Follow these handy hints for exam success:

EXAMINER'S SECRET

If you cannot choose between two questions, jot down a plan for each to help you decide – it may be that what appeared to be the most straightforward question is more difficult than you thought.

EXAMINER'S SECRET

To do well, you do not have to write at great length: you can get the highest marks with an essay of two sides.

BEFORE YOU START

- Make sure you know the subject of the examination so that you are properly prepared and equipped.
- You need to be comfortable and free from distractions. Inform the invigilator if anything is off-putting, e.g. a shaky desk.
- Read the instructions, or rubric, on the front of the examination paper. You should know by now what you have to do but check to reassure yourself.
- Observe the time allocation – and follow it carefully. If they recommend 60 minutes for Question 1 and 30 minutes for Question 2, it is because Question 1 carries twice as many marks.
- Consider the mark allocation. You should write a longer response for 4 marks than for 2 marks.

WRITING YOUR RESPONSES

- Use the questions to structure your response, e.g. question: 'The endings of X's poems are always particularly significant. Explain their importance with reference to two poems.' The first part of your answer will describe the ending of the first poem; the second part will look at the ending of the second poem; the third part will be an explanation of the significance of the two endings.

- Write a brief draft outline of your response.
- A typical 30-minute examination essay is probably between 400 and 600 words in length.
- Keep your writing legible and easy to read, using paragraphs to show the structure of your answers.
- Spend a couple of minutes afterwards quickly checking for obvious errors.

Always read the whole examination paper before you start writing.

WHEN YOU HAVE FINISHED

- Don't be downhearted – if you found the examination difficult, it is probably because you really worked at the questions. Let's face it, they are not meant to be easy!
- Don't pay too much attention to what your friends have to say about the paper. Everyone's experience is different and no two people ever give the same answers.

IMPROVE YOUR GRADE

A good essay will show you understand various aspects of the play. You will need to show that you have a good knowledge of the plot or the story-line of the play, the order in which things happen and the way the events are organised.

You should show you understand how the characters are revealed to us by what they do, what they say and what others say about them, their relationships to each other and how they change in the course of the play.

In the course of the play, the playwright will create a particular atmosphere through the way the stage is lit, the furnishings on the stage, the way characters react to each other, the use of special effects. You should be aware of how these things affect or reflect what is happening.

Plan your answers then you won't repeat yourself.

Writers are influenced by what has already happened, what is happening in their lives and by what they hope, or fear, may happen in the future. In their writing they may reflect or contradict the views, opinions and beliefs of other people. You should consider the writer's views and comment on the social and historical context in which the writer was working.

IMPROVING YOUR RESPONSE FROM A D TO A C

In awarding your essay a D Grade the examiner will have considered that you:

- Showed understanding of the different layers of meaning in the play
- Made useful points which you supported with textual evidence
- Showed understanding of the social conditions at the time in which the play was set
- Showed understanding of the culture at the time the play was set

You will also have shown him that you **understand**:

- Some of the dramatic effects of what the characters did and said
- The effect created by the structure of the play and the dramatic devices that the playwright used

The **key word** for recognising a D Grade is **understand.**

To raise your Grade to a C you need to show the examiner that you:

EXAMINER'S SECRET

Try to convey the sense of comedy/drama experienced by a real audience.

- Have insight into how the playwright puts his different meanings and ideas across through the language and the structure of the play
- Can use appropriate details to support your views
- Can set out your ideas in effective ways
- Can write clearly about how the historical, cultural and social setting affects our understanding of the play

You will have also shown **insight into**:

- The dramatic effects of the characters and the action
- The effects of the dramatic devices and the structure of the play

The **key word** for recognising a C Grade is **insight.**

For example, instead of writing **'When Gerald first meets the girl in the bar of the Palace Music Hall Theatre he finds her attractive'**, you can say:

> **When Gerald first sees Daisy Renton in the bar of the Palace Music Hall, she is with 'women of the town', but Gerald notices her because she seems so different from the other women. Priestley highlights the difference between the girl and the other women. Gerald's description of her reminds us of the way that both Mr Birling and Sheila had described Eva Smith, and this links the two girls.**

Be selective with your quotations, and if possible try to make cross-references with other parts of the play.

IMPROVING YOUR RESPONSE TO AN A/A*

To raise your Grade to an A/A* Grade you have to show that you:

- Have written clearly argued responses which are:

  Original

  Coherent

  Enthusiastic

  Sensitive
- Can analyse and interpret the importance of such things as the social and historical setting of the play
- Can analyse and interpret the cultural and literary tradition from which the writer comes

You will also have shown an original approach when analysing and interpreting:

- The dramatic effects created by the characters – by what they say, by what they do, and by what happens to them
- The way the playwright structures his play – the way things lead on from each other and where he puts in particularly dramatic moments or develops particular themes

Higher-level achievement begins at the point when you show you are aware of being marked.

- The playwright's use of dramatic devices including lighting changes, the sort of set that appears on the stage, the use of particular sorts of language.

The **key words** here are **originality**, **analysis** and **interpretation**.

Now you might be developing your earlier statement about Gerald's meeting with the girl so it looks something like this:

When Gerald first meets the girl she is in the bar of the Palace Variety Theatre among 'women of the town'. Gerald's polite use of the euphemism maintains his gentlemanly qualities, although it reminds us that young men were likely to break out 'and have a bit of fun' in Edwardian society just as Mr Birling's generation had done during Victorian times. Gerald describes the girl as 'very pretty', and his gentle recollection of her 'soft brown hair and big dark eyes' causes him to break down as he is struck by the full realisation of her death. From Gerald's description it is clear that he finds her attractive. She does not seem to belong there, she stands out from the 'hard-eyed dough-faced women' and we are reminded of the way that both Mr Birling and Sheila have described Eva Smith. It is her sacking from Birlings and then from Milwards which has forced her to become Daisy Renton and to 'lead a different sort of life'. Priestley forges these links so that we begin to suspect that whatever happens between her and Gerald will be another link that helps lead to her moral decline and, eventually, to her suicide.

EXAMINER'S SECRET

A candidate who is capable of arriving at unusual, well-supported judgements *independently* is likely to receive the highest marks.

In this answer you will be showing you can interpret and analyse Priestley's intentions. Instead of just making a statement about a character and an event, you have interpreted the character's motives, analysed the language Priestley uses and you have linked the event to what has gone before and to what may follow. You are not simply observing, but presenting a line of thought which explores the language, the characters and the events of the play against the social and cultural background of the time in which it is set.

You may be thinking that some (or even all!) of this sounds a bit beyond you. Don't worry – have a go at planning, preparing, developing and checking your answer really carefully and you might be in for a very pleasant surprise!

SAMPLE ESSAY PLAN

A typical essay question on *An Inspector Calls* is followed by a sample essay plan in note form. This does not present the only answer to the question, merely one answer. Do not be afraid to include your own ideas, and leave out some of those in the sample! Remember that quotations are essential to prove and illustrate the points you make.

To what extent can Gerald Croft be held responsible for the death of Eva Smith/Daisy Renton?

Such a question anticipates a wide-ranging response. Let us suppose that you feel that Gerald does bear considerable responsibility for the death of the girl. To answer the question 'to what extent' you will have to put his role in context.

PART 1

A description of Gerald Croft, his background and his relationship with the Birling family.

PART 2

How his relationship with the girl is revealed, his desire to keep the relationship secret, where he met the girl, why he noticed her, how the relationship developed, and how the relationship ended.

PART 3

An examination of his motives – to rescue a pretty girl in trouble, to offer food and shelter to someone who was vulnerable. His reaction to the affection that the girl's gratitude generated. Your decision on whether his motives were honourable a) when he first met the girl, b) when he offered her accommodation, c) when he made her his mistress and d) when he left her.

PART 4

EXAMINER'S SECRET

You are always given credit for writing your essay plans.

Where Gerald's association with the girl fits in with the girl's contact with the other characters: what each had done: how the links of the chain fit together.

PART 5

The girl had been happy with Gerald, so he had given her something worthwhile in her life. How Gerald's treatment contrasts with the treatment of others, how he improved the quality of her life. But that, after he left her, her life was so much worse.

PART 6: CONCLUSION

That Gerald might be the only one that even the Inspector admits made her happy for a time, but he let her down as much as anyone else, perhaps more so since he gave her a little happiness and then took it away, leaving her at the mercy of people like Eric – a younger version of Alderman Meggarty. Gerald's support of Mr Birling over the sacking of the girl from the factory, his lead in disproving the authenticity of the Inspector and his telephone call to the Infirmary, his willingness to believe that since there was no dead girl then there was no need to feel guilty or troubled – shown by his instant request to Sheila to take back the ring, all suggest that he has not learnt a lesson and must take at least an equal share of the guilt.
This is by no means an exhaustive or definitive answer to the question. However, looked at in conjunction with the general notes above, it does show you the way your mind should be working in order to produce a reasonably thorough essay.

FURTHER QUESTIONS

Make a plan as shown above and attempt these questions.

1. Which of the characters is most affected by the events of the evening?
2. How is *An Inspector Calls* different from a typical detective thriller?

3. Examine the evidence to decide whether Eva Smith and Daisy Renton are indeed one and the same person.
4. How does the play show up the contrast between the philosophies of Arthur Birling and Inspector Goole?
5. What aspects of British society does the play criticise?
6. How are Gerald and Eric's relationships with the girl different?
7. Examine how the play's historical setting might affect a modern audience's response to and appreciation of the play and its ideas.
8. Describe the way that Priestley develops Sheila's character during the course of the play.
9. Is there anything about Mrs Birling's character, attitudes or behaviour that arouses our sympathy?
10. How does Priestley reveal his views about responsibility? Do you think he gets his message across successfully?

Now take a break! 

coup de theatre a sudden and spectacular turn of events in the plot of a play

dialogue speech and conversation between characters

didactic writing or speech intended to teach or instruct

dramatic irony this occurs when the development of the plot allows the audience to possess more information about what is happening than some of the characters have themselves

euphemism unpleasant, embarrassing or frightening facts or words can be concealed behind a 'euphemism' – a word or phrase less blunt or offensive

hyperbole a figure of speech in which emphasis is achieved by exaggeration

irony this consists of saying one thing while you mean another, often through understatement, concealment or indirect statement

monologue lengthy speech by one person

morality play form of play developed in the late Middle Ages in which a Christian moral lesson was brought out through the struggle between the forces of good and evil

polemic a piece of writing expressing an argument about important social issues such as religion or politics

sarcasm an extreme form of irony, usually intended to be hurtful

stage directions advice printed in the text of a play giving instructions or information about the movements, gestures and appearance of the actors, or on the special effects required at a particular moment in the action

the unities in Classical Greek drama, plays conformed to the unities of action and time – one complete action happening in a single day or night. The unity of place was added later

well-made play a play that exhibits a neatness of plot and smooth-functioning exactness of action, with all its parts fitting together precisely. *An Inspector Calls* works through an interlocking series of unexpected discourses, leading up to a final revelation that is almost a trick ending

whodunnit a novel, play etc concerned with crime, usually a murder

CHECKPOINT HINTS/ANSWERS

CHECKPOINT 1

- Birling first says that the engagement makes him happy and he expresses the hope that the couple will make each other happy.
- He says that the event has brought the families together and may bring the family businesses together, giving them greater profits.
- He convinces himself that talk of war, industrial trouble or financial hardship is nonsense.
- He knows the right things to say, but can't help looking at life in business terms.

CHECKPOINT 2

- He is a self-important man.
- He has a strong belief in his own position of power.
- He wants to be accepted into society and is proud of his humble start in life.
- He has a narrow view of the world.
- He prefers to believe what suits his purpose.

CHECKPOINT 3

- Birling's comments to Gerald are warmer in tone.
- He seems to dismiss Eric as being irrelevant.
- He confides his secret, about the possible knighthood, to Gerald.
- He shares jokes with Gerald.
- His tone towards Eric is harsher and almost shows contempt.
- Later Gerald shares Birling's views on the strike and on sacking the ringleaders, but Eric thinks his father has been too harsh.

CHECKPOINT 4

- The Inspector uses the expression 'a chain of events' (Act I, p. 14) quite early on.
- The method of questioning each member of the family in turn adds to this sense of a chain.
- The deliberate mention of when each event happens links what one character has done to the next one questioned.
- There are aspects of the girl's description, manner or behaviour that are common to more than one character's memory of her.

CHECKPOINT 5

Birling:

- Tells the Inspector he has been an alderman, Lord Mayor and a magistrate
- Mentions his friendship with the Chief Constable
- Threatens to report the Inspector for 'uncalled-for and officious' (Act I, p. 17) behaviour

Mrs Birling:

- Attempts to dismiss the Inspector
- Patronises the Inspector who has 'made a great impression on this child' (Act II, p. 30) (Sheila) but clearly not on her
- Calls the Inspector 'impertinent' (Act II, p. 30) and says he is behaving in 'a rather peculiar and offensive manner' (Act II, p. 31)
- Points out Birling's social position as a magistrate and former Lord Mayor

CHECKPOINT 6

The Inspector says that:

- She died in the Infirmary after swallowing disinfectant.
- She had left a letter, a photograph and a diary.
- She had used more than one name.
- She had been employed in Birling's factory and been sacked in September 1910 for asking for higher wages.
- Her parents were both dead.
- She had been out of work for two months, had no savings and was becoming desperate.

- Had got a job in Milwards shop, but been sacked in January 1911 after a customer had complained.
- She had changed her name to Daisy Renton and had decided to try another kind of life.

CHECKPOINT 7

- Birling dealt with all the strike leaders in the same way.
- There was nothing personal in Birling's behaviour.
- It was not considered unusual for strikers to be dealt with harshly.
- Birling acts from a view of business, Sheila acts out of spite and jealousy.
- Sheila picks on a stranger who is weaker than she is.
- Sheila's actions are out of proportion to whatever she thinks the girl has done.

CHECKPOINT 8

- Sheila was very happy earlier in the evening.
- She has been touched by the Inspector's description of the dead girl.
- She has condemned her father's treatment of the girl and now realises that she has been equally guilty.

CHECKPOINT 9

- Sheila's carefree attitude has been shaken.
- Gerald has witnessed her confessing to shameful behaviour.
- She has noticed Gerald looking at her in an accusing way.
- She is prepared to defend herself by suggesting Gerald has 'done things you're ashamed of too' (Act I, p. 23).
- Sheila notices Gerald's guilt when the name of Daisy Renton is mentioned.
- Sheila is upset when she connects Gerald's lack of attention to her in the summer with his relationship with Daisy Renton.

CHECKPOINT 10

- He decides who will be questioned and when.
- He decides who will or will not see the photograph.
- He makes Arthur Birling recognise the implications of others possibly being involved in the 'chain of events' (Act I, p. 14).
- He contradicts Birling and overrules his wish that Sheila should leave the room.
- His method of questioning draws confessions from Birling and Sheila.
- He stops the potential argument between Sheila and Gerald.
- He makes it clear he will not leave until he gets to 'know all that happened' (Act I, p. 25).
- His way of dropping in the name of Daisy Renton catches Gerald out.

CHECKPOINT 11

- When Sheila returns she says 'You knew it was me all the time, didn't you?' (Act I, p. 22).
- Sheila is convinced that 'he knows' (Act I, p. 26) what they have done before they tell him.
- She believes he knows things that they themselves do not know yet.

CHECKPOINT 12

Birling:

- Is reluctant to discuss his business
- Refuses to see that he has done wrong
- Is unmoved by the girl's death
- Has little concern for what might have happened to the girl after he sacked her
- Is casual about the idea that the girl may have had to 'Go on the streets' (Act I, p. 16)

- Was concerned only about his business and his profits

Gerald:

- Tells the story fully, after a brief attempt at denying knowledge of the girl
- Is clearly distressed when the fact of the girl's death sinks in
- Does not blame the girl for what happened between them
- Stresses the girl's good points
- Shows care and compassion in his tone
- Recognises how important he became to her
- Admits she behaved better than he did

CHECKPOINT 13

- She admits she disliked Gerald after his reactions to her own confession and her realisation that he had had a relationship with the girl.
- She says she now respects him more and acknowledges he has been honest.
- She accepts his motives were originally good ones and she recognises that by revealing their secrets each now sees the other in a new light.

CHECKPOINT 14

- The photograph is used to jog Arthur Birling's memory.
- It is used to shock Sheila.
- It is used to show Mrs Birling up as a liar.
- As Gerald points out, the photograph is only seen by one person at a time.
- There is no way of knowing if they all saw the same photograph.

CHECKPOINT 15

- She talks down to Sheila and to the Inspector and looks down on those, like the girl, who are in trouble.
- She calls the Inspector 'impertinent' (Act II, p. 30).
- She speaks '*haughtily*' (Act II, p. 30), '*grandly*' (Act II, p. 31) and '*sharply*' (Act II, p. 32).
- She claims to have done nothing wrong and tries to pass the blame on to anyone other than herself.
- She says the girl has only herself to blame.
- She says, of the father of the unborn child, 'If the girl's death is due to anybody, then it's due to him' (Act II, p. 48).
- She admits to being prejudiced.

CHECKPOINT 16

- He is described as being young.
- He is 'silly and wild' (Act II, p. 46) and we have seen Eric being silly at the dinner party.
- He drinks too much and is a 'drunken young idler' (Act II, p. 48).
- He was of a different social class from the girl.

CHECKPOINT 17

Gerald:

- Rescued her from a drunken man who was forcing his attentions onto her
- Gave her a better life, at least for a time
- Showed real friendship and affection
- Is not sure if he loved her but recognises the possibility that he could have done
- Helped her honestly from his own resources

Eric:

- Was drunk and forced himself on her
- Uses the girl for his own selfish pleasure
- There is no warmth or friendship; he doesn't even know her name
- Made her pregnant and tried to use stolen money to help her.

CHECKPOINT 18

- Birling emphasises the importance of business and money.
- He highlights a prosperous situation for a small number of people.
- He does not recognise any sense of responsibility on the part of employers for the well-being of those who work for them.
- He forecasts 'a very good time' (Act I, p. 6) ahead and discounts talk of war and bloodshed. He pins his hopes on the advantages that technology will bring.
- He sees social reformers as 'cranks' (Act I, p. 10).
- The Inspector highlights the poor conditions suffered by so many.
- He stresses 'We are members of one body' (Act III, p. 56) so we are dependent on each other.
- He warns that if changes are not made the future will be one of 'fire and blood and anguish' (Act III, p. 56).

CHECKPOINT 19

- Sheila feels it makes no difference. She recognises that they have all done wrong. She feels that he was their inspector (that is, he inspected their behaviour) whether he was a policeman or not.
- Eric supports Sheila. He sees the need for them to change their behaviour.
- Mr Birling sees that if the Inspector is not a real policeman then there is less chance of a scandal over their dealings with the girl. He foresees no scandal relating to the money stolen from the firm's office. He persuades himself it has all been a trick, 'an elaborate sell' (Act III, p. 70).
- Mrs Birling supports her husband. She feels that if the Inspector was an impostor then she has been right to behave as she has.
- Gerald is excited by the prospect that there has not been any official investigation. He appears to believe that the Inspector being a fake puts things right.

CHECKPOINT 20

- Sheila and Eric accept responsibility.
- They do not feel that anything has happened to relieve their guilt.
- They realise the seriousness of their actions and have taken the Inspector's message to heart.
- They have an understanding that they need to change their behaviour in the future.
- Priestley uses these two as symbols of the hope for a better future that lies in a younger generation.

TEST YOURSELF (ACT I)

1 Mr Birling
2 The Inspector
3 Mr Birling
4 Sheila
5 Gerald
6 Mr Birling
7 Sheila

TEST YOURSELF (ACT II)

1 Sheila
2 Mrs Birling
3 The Inspector
4 Mrs Birling
5 Sheila
6 Gerald
7 Gerald

TEST YOURSELF (ACT III)

1 Eric
2 The Inspector
3 Sheila
4 Mrs Birling
5 Sheila
6 Eric
7 Mrs Birling

NOTES

Notes

Notes

Notes

York Notes for GCSE

Maya Angelou
I Know Why the Caged Bird Sings

Jane Austen
Pride and Prejudice

Alan Ayckbourn
Absent Friends

Elizabeth Barrett Browning
Selected Poems

Robert Bolt
A Man for All Seasons

Harold Brighouse
Hobson's Choice

Charlotte Brontë
Jane Eyre

Emily Brontë
Wuthering Heights

Shelagh Delaney
A Taste of Honey

Charles Dickens
David Copperfield
Great Expectations
Hard Times
Oliver Twist

Roddy Doyle
Paddy Clarke Ha Ha Ha

George Eliot
Silas Marner
The Mill on the Floss

Anne Frank
The Diary of a Young Girl

William Golding
Lord of the Flies

Oliver Goldsmith
She Stoops to Conquer

Willis Hall
The Long and the Short and the Tall

Thomas Hardy
Far from the Madding Crowd
The Mayor of Casterbridge
Tess of the d'Urbervilles
The Withered Arm and other Wessex Tales

L.P. Hartley
The Go-Between

Seamus Heaney
Selected Poems

Susan Hill
I'm the King of the Castle

Barry Hines
A Kestrel for a Knave

Louise Lawrence
Children of the Dust

Harper Lee
To Kill a Mockingbird

Laurie Lee
Cider with Rosie

Arthur Miller
The Crucible
A View from the Bridge

Robert O'Brien
Z for Zachariah

Frank O'Connor
My Oedipus Complex and Other Stories

George Orwell
Animal Farm

J.B. Priestley
An Inspector Calls
When We Are Married

Willy Russell
Educating Rita
Our Day Out

J.D. Salinger
The Catcher in the Rye

William Shakespeare
Henry IV Part 1
Henry V
Julius Caesar
Macbeth
The Merchant of Venice
A Midsummer Night's Dream
Much Ado About Nothing
Romeo and Juliet
The Tempest
Twelfth Night

George Bernard Shaw
Pygmalion

Mary Shelley
Frankenstein

R.C. Sherriff
Journey's End

Rukshana Smith
Salt on the snow

John Steinbeck
Of Mice and Men

Robert Louis Stevenson
Dr Jekyll and Mr Hyde

Jonathan Swift
Gulliver's Travels

Robert Swindells
Daz 4 Zoe

Mildred D. Taylor
Roll of Thunder, Hear My Cry

Mark Twain
Huckleberry Finn

James Watson
Talking in Whispers

Edith Wharton
Ethan Frome

William Wordsworth
Selected Poems

A Choice of Poets

Mystery Stories of the Nineteenth Century including The Signalman

Nineteenth Century Short Stories

Poetry of the First World War

Six Women Poets

YORK NOTES ADVANCED

Margaret Atwood
Cat's Eye
The Handmaid's Tale

Jane Austen
Emma
Mansfield Park
Persuasion
Pride and Prejudice
Sense and Sensibility

Alan Bennett
Talking Heads

William Blake
Songs of Innocence and of Experience

Charlotte Brontë
Jane Eyre
Villette

Emily Brontë
Wuthering Heights

Angela Carter
Nights at the Circus

Geoffrey Chaucer
The Franklin's Prologue and Tale
The Miller's Prologue and Tale
The Prologue to the Canterbury Tales
The Wife of Bath's Prologue and Tale

Samuel Coleridge
Selected Poems

Joseph Conrad
Heart of Darkness

Daniel Defoe
Moll Flanders

Charles Dickens
Bleak House
Great Expectations
Hard Times

Emily Dickinson
Selected Poems

John Donne
Selected Poems

Carol Ann Duffy
Selected Poems

George Eliot
Middlemarch
The Mill on the Floss

T.S. Eliot
Selected Poems
The Waste Land

F. Scott Fitzgerald
The Great Gatsby

E.M. Forster
A Passage to India

Brian Friel
Translations

Thomas Hardy
Jude the Obscure
The Mayor of Casterbridge
The Return of the Native
Selected Poems
Tess of the d'Urbervilles

Seamus Heaney
Selected Poems from 'Opened Ground'

Nathaniel Hawthorne
The Scarlet Letter

Homer
The Iliad
The Odyssey

Aldous Huxley
Brave New World

Kazuo Ishiguro
The Remains of the Day

Ben Jonson
The Alchemist

James Joyce
Dubliners

John Keats
Selected Poems

Christopher Marlowe
Doctor Faustus
Edward II

Arthur Miller
Death of a Salesman

John Milton
Paradise Lost Books I & II

Toni Morrison
Beloved

George Orwell
Nineteen Eighty-Four

Sylvia Plath
Selected Poems

Alexander Pope
Rape of the Lock & Selected Poems

William Shakespeare
Antony and Cleopatra
As You Like It
Hamlet
Henry IV Part I
King Lear
Macbeth
Measure for Measure
The Merchant of Venice
A Midsummer Night's Dream
Much Ado About Nothing
Othello
Richard II
Richard III
Romeo and Juliet
The Taming of the Shrew
The Tempest
Twelfth Night
The Winter's Tale

George Bernard Shaw
Saint Joan

Mary Shelley
Frankenstein

Jonathan Swift
Gulliver's Travels and A Modest Proposal

Alfred Tennyson
Selected Poems

Virgil
The Aeneid

Alice Walker
The Color Purple

Oscar Wilde
The Importance of Being Earnest

Tennessee Williams
A Streetcar Named Desire

Jeanette Winterson
Oranges Are Not the Only Fruit

John Webster
The Duchess of Malfi

Virginia Woolf
To the Lighthouse

W.B. Yeats
Selected Poems

Metaphysical Poets

THE ULTIMATE WEB SITE FOR THE ULTIMATE LITERATURE GUIDES

At York Notes we believe in helping you achieve exam success. Log on to **www.yorknotes.com** and see how we have made revision even easier, with over 300 titles available to download twenty-four hours a day. The downloads have lots of additional features such as pop-up boxes providing instant glossary definitions, user-friendly links to every part of the guide, and scanned illustrations offering visual appeal. All you need to do is log on to **www.yorknotes.com** and download the books you need to help you achieve exam success.

KEY FEATURES:

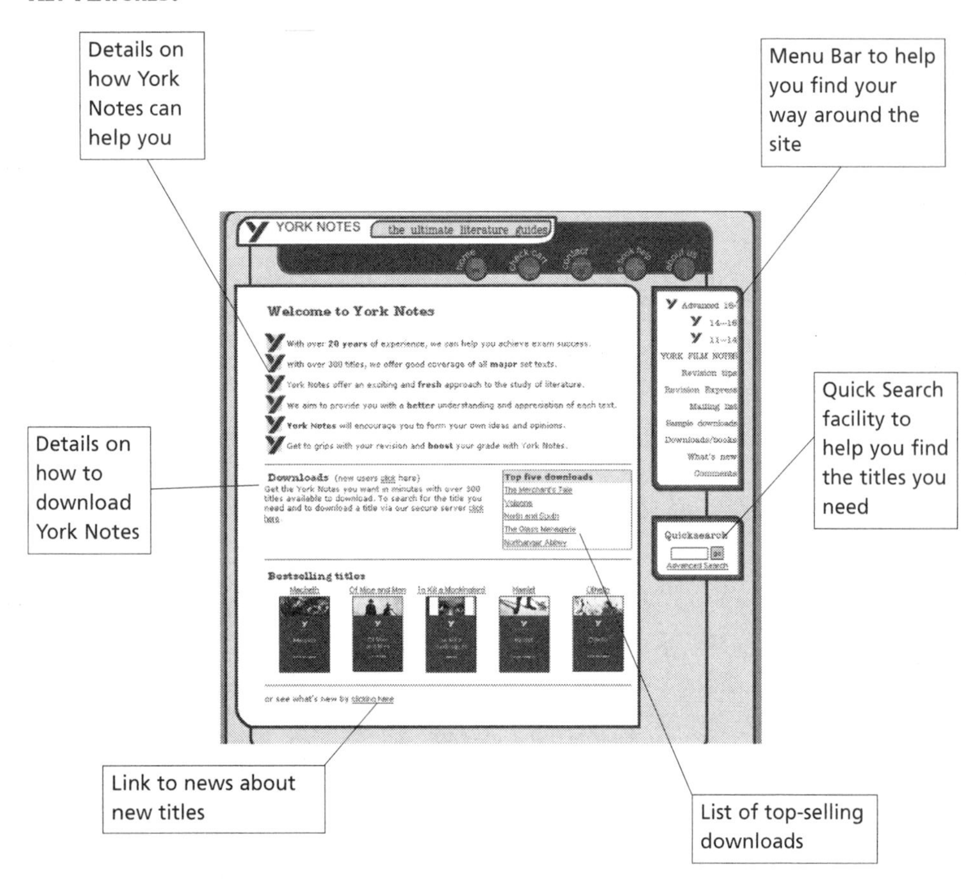